The Ethics of
Capital Punishment

DATE DUE CR 2006

Other books in the At Issue series:

The Ethics of Capital Punishment

Nick Fisanick, *Book Editor*

Bruce Glassman, *Vice President*
Bonnie Szumski, *Publisher*
Helen Cothran, *Managing Editor*

GREENHAVEN PRESS
An imprint of Thomson Gale, a part of The Thomson Corporation

THOMSON
✶
GALE

Detroit • New York • San Francisco • San Diego • New Haven, Conn.
Waterville, Maine • London • Munich

For more information, contact
Greenhaven Press
27500 Drake Rd.
Farmington Hills, MI 48331-3535
Or you can visit our Internet site at http://www.gale.com

LIBRARY OF CONGRESS CATALOGING-IN-PUBLICATION DATA
The ethics of capital punishment / Nick Fisanick, book editor.
p. cm. — (At issue)
Includes bibliographical references and index.
ISBN 0-7377-2338-6 (lib. : alk. paper) — ISBN 0-7377-2339-4 (pbk. : alk. paper)
1. Capital punishment—United States. 2. Capital punishment—Moral and ethical aspects. I. Fisanick, Nick. II. At issue (San Diego, Calif.)
HV8699.U5E84 2005
179.7—dc22   2004054352

Printed in the United States of America

Contents

Introduction

One of the most significant developments in the current debate over capital punishment came in January 2000, when Illinois governor George Ryan imposed an unprecedented, open-ended moratorium on his state's death penalty. His announcement came eleven months after Anthony Porter, whose execution Ryan would have presided over, was exonerated of the murder he had been convicted of in 1982. (A group of journalism students at Northwestern University had amassed clear evidence that Porter was innocent, including a videotaped confession from the real killer.) Porter was the thirteenth death row inmate to be exonerated in Illinois since the state had reinstated the death penalty in 1976; only twelve people had been executed in that time. Ryan—who came to office as a pro–capital punishment candidate—was troubled that the state's criminal justice system was wrongly sentencing people to death. In explaining the moratorium, he said, "Until I can be sure with moral certainty that no innocent man or woman is facing a lethal injection," he announced, "no one will meet that fate."

An ethical dilemma

Ryan's decision was hailed as a major victory by opponents of capital punishment. However, it is interesting to note that Ryan did not take issue with the belief that death is a justifiable punishment for some crimes. In fact, in making his announcement, Ryan clarified his views, stating, "I still believe the death penalty is a proper response to heinous crimes. . . . But I want to make sure . . . that the person who is put to death is absolutely guilty." Ryan's moratorium was not based on the belief that capital punishment is morally wrong; rather, he objected to the way it was applied in his state.

The turning point for Ryan came a few weeks after Porter's exoneration: Ryan had to decide whether to authorize another execution, this time in the case of Andrew Kokoraleis, who had been convicted of raping and murdering a twenty-one-year-old woman. "This was a horrible crime, and I am the father of five

7

daughters," Ryan later explained in an interview, "But after the mistakes the system had made with Porter, I wasn't sure what to do. I agonized. I checked and double-checked and triple-checked the facts. . . . It was the most emotional experience I have ever been through in my life." In the Kokoraleis case, Ryan went ahead with the execution, but in the next three months, two more death row inmates were exonerated. When the Illinois state attorney general called seeking another execution, Ryan initiated the moratorium.

The agonizing deliberation that Ryan experienced contrasts sharply with the polarized views of many Americans have about the death penalty. As death penalty opponent Stephen Nathanson explains,

> One side thinks that respect for life forbids the use of the death penalty, while the other believes that respect for life requires it. For many people on both sides of the debate, the issue is simple and clear-cut, and they find it difficult to understand how anyone could see things differently.

Those involved in the criminal justice system, including governors such as Ryan, must consider issues beyond the "respect for life" dichotomy that Nathanson describes. They must consider not just whether capital punishment is justified in the abstract, but whether the criminal justice system that they are responsible for is operating in a fair and just manner. The Illinois moratorium shows how difficult it can be to separate one's moral beliefs about whether the death penalty is justified from judgments about the fairness of the criminal justice system in applying the penalty. Two ethical principles—retributivism and utilitarianism—are key to understanding both the dilemma that Ryan faced and the broader debate over capital punishment.

The ethics of capital punishment

According to Louis P. Pojman, a prominent advocate for capital punishment, "Retributivism is the theory that the criminal *deserves* to be punished and deserves to be punished in proportion to the gravity of his or her crime." This idea is often expressed with the biblical phrase "an eye for an eye," though a more fitting biblical quotation might be Genesis 9:6, "Who so sheddeth man's blood, by man shall his blood be shed." One of the most frequent arguments of death penalty supporters is that a person who commits murder forfeits his or her right to live and deserves to die.] In this retributive view, the death penalty is a necessary means of achieving justice.

Death penalty opponents do not necessarily reject the concept of retributive punishment, but they do reject the idea that capital punishment is necessary to achieve retribution. Many death penalty opponents believe that support for the death penalty is based on vengeance—which stems from anger—rather than retribution—which is based on justice. As death penalty opponent John D. Bessler writes, "As far as I can tell, vengeance is, and always has been, the main driving force behind executions." Death penalty opponents generally argue that life imprisonment is a better punishment than capital punishment.

The second major ethical framework through which to view the ethics of capital punishment is utilitarianism. According to this philosophy, the right action is the one that provides the most benefits for the greatest number of people. Whereas retributivism says that punishment is necessary to achieve justice, utilitarianism says that punishment is only justified if it achieves socially desirable effects.

Both sides of the capital punishment debate employ utilitarian arguments. For example, opponents of the death penalty often talk about a cycle of suffering and violence, noting that executions cause suffering to the families of the executed, may traumatize those who order and carry out the execution, and may desensitize the public at large to the act of killing. In contrast, utilitarian supporters of capital punishment may argue that it brings a sense of peace and closure to the families of the victims.

One of the most important utilitarian arguments for the death penalty is that of deterrence. According to this argument, capital punishment is ethically justified not because it is an appropriate punishment but because it helps prevent murders and other crimes. As conservative writer William Tucker argues, "The remarkable thing about the death penalty is why anyone would think it doesn't deter murder. No one wants to die. Why wouldn't the fear of death make [would-be murderers] think twice?" There is an enormous amount of research and literature for and against the deterrence argument; much of it focuses on statistics and criminology rather than ethics, but the underlying principle is a utilitarian one.

While proponents of capital punishment focus on the deterrence argument, opponents are quick to raise the concern that prompted Ryan's moratorium—the possibility that a given state's system of capital punishment could result in the execution of innocent people. When death penalty opponents argue that capital punishment should be banned, not because it is inherently immoral, but because it could lead to the execution of innocent people, they are making a utilitarian argument.

For the true utilitarian, however, the possibility that innocent people could be executed is not a strong enough reason to reject capital punishment. Instead one must weigh all of the other positive and negative effects that capital punishment has on society. Indeed, utilitarian arguments about capital punishment can become very complicated because utilitarians seek to weigh *all* the effects of capital punishment to determine whether it is justified or not.

Ethics in practice

Retributive justice calls for strict punishment; utilitarianism calls for careful deliberation about the effects of punishment. Both ethical frameworks inform the debate over capital punishment. However, most people do not adhere strictly to one principle or the other, instead using a combination of both philosophies—as well as other principles and their own personal beliefs—when faced with an ethical problem.

George Ryan's belief in retributive justice led him to support the death penalty, and later a utilitarian analysis of his state's system of capital punishment caused him to alter his position. His ethical reasoning and decision to institute a moratorium generated a great deal of controversy. Many death penalty opponents disagreed with Ryan's reasoning but applauded his final decision, just as many supporters of capital punishment believe that Ryan should have worked to reform the Illinois criminal justice system without imposing his moratorium. However one views Ryan's decision, it serves as an excellent demonstration of how the issue of capital punishment often presents people—even those with strong opinions on justice, the value of life, and the role of government—with ethical dilemmas.

1

Executions Are Only Just If They Meet Stringent Moral Conditions

Lloyd Steffen

Lloyd Steffen is a professor of religious studies and university chaplain at Lehigh University in Bethlehem, Pennsylvania. He is the author of Executing Justice.

Capital punishment is a form of killing that is only used when someone has committed an extremely serious crime. In order to preserve justice for society, the legal system must ensure that strict moral and ethical conditions are met before it imposes an execution. The crime, the accused, and those implementing the punishment must be carefully scrutinized before an execution can be deemed just.

A theory of just execution would establish that in light of a moral presumption against capital punishment, an execution could not proceed unless that presumption were lifted. That presumption could only be lifted—and an execution justified—if the requirements of justice were met and the safeguards that ensure justice were preserved. The following criteria serve to indicate what would be required to justify lifting the moral presumption against capital punishment, and, as in other "presumption/exception" theories, such as "just war" or "just abortion," all of the criteria have to be met. Failure to satisfy all the criteria would block the effort to lift the presumption, so that moral permissibility would necessarily fail to at-

Lloyd Steffen, *Executing Justice*. Cleveland, OH: Pilgrim Press, 1998. Copyright © 1998 by Lloyd Steffen.

tach to capital punishment or, more precisely, to particular instances of it.

Legitimate authority

In order for an execution to be deemed just, it must be imposed by legitimate authority. Execution must be authorized and sanctioned as a tool in a state's justice system. This requirement prohibits vigilantism or any extralegal execution by mob violence or terrorism. The extralegal practice of lynching so common in the United States, which did not have a lynching-free year until 1953, is rendered morally impermissible. The point of this criterion is to assure that no criminal act that has deprived a person of life be punished by a private citizen or citizens. In the political commonwealth governed by a rule of law, it is the law, not the individual victims of crime or their families or clans, that determines how a response shall be made to a criminal offender, the theory being that the harm committed in political society is not only to the immediate victim of crime but to the state itself. Capital punishment, to be morally just, must therefore be imposed under the rule of law and in the name of the collective will of the sovereign power. It is the sovereign power that justly authorizes capital punishment through a legal system of justice administration, and this is the case even though appeals for moral justification are sometimes referred out of the authority of the legal system to a religious source of sanction and legitimation. But even when appeal is made to a source of religious legitimation for the death penalty, it is clear that the particulars of any given case where it is believed the religious sanction would apply are determined by some kind of legal system that exercises, on behalf of the religious sanction, sovereign power—or else God (or whatever transcendent or ultimate religious source is in question) could simply effect the execution directly without any delegating of the divine will to human agents.

Just cause

A just cause for imposing the death penalty must be claimed in order to justify using it. Just cause can be established by considering the nature of the crime itself and applying a principle of proportionality so that extreme crimes would be met with extreme punishments. The death penalty is an extreme penalty.

Resorting to the death penalty would be justified under this criterion as an extreme but proportionate response to an extreme offense. This criterion takes account of an "evolving standard of decency," as the phrase has found its way into American law, so that the tendency would be to restrict the extreme penalty to truly extreme crimes, such as aggravated murder. Executing a person for stealing a calf—the first crime in America that brought about a death sentence and an execution—or for any of the larcenies that legally called for the death penalty in the societies of [philosophers John] Locke, [Immanuel] Kant, and John Stuart Mill no longer meets this test. Such crimes lack sufficient gravity to establish just cause. Practically speaking, only a very restricted class of crimes—murder and perhaps treason—are thus considered justly eligible for the death penalty, and then only the gravest instances of offense within that class.

> *Against that threat, society, acting on the behalf of the welfare of all, has a right to protect itself.*

But focus on the nature of the crime itself does not exhaust the just cause criterion. And it ought not to, since what does—and what does not—constitute a "gravest of the grave" crime will always be subject to a relativistic interpretation. Although it is beyond dispute that we who are members of the moral community today consider Daniell Frank's execution in 1622 for the crime of stealing a calf unjust and disproportionate, it clearly was not beyond dispute in the moral community of 1622 Colonial America. Stealing a calf was just cause for hanging. If just cause were to be determined only by appealing to what a society held at any given moment to be a crime sufficiently grave to establish just cause, we would have to conclude that justice was served by the execution of Daniell Frank in 1622, even though that execution offends our modern standards of decency. And these standards would then be subject to such contextualization themselves, for we could situate the American penchant for execution within the wider context of the family of nations.

Although countries that have poor records of respecting human rights still employ the death penalty—Saudi Arabia,

Iran, Iraq, and China come to mind—the fact is that most nations that Americans would identify as affirming values that correspond to our own have abolished the death penalty, which means this: that on the basis of an "evolving standard of decency," the death penalty *even for murder—even aggravated murder—has been abolished as failing to satisfy just cause.* Were we to determine just cause by such a relativistic mode of evaluation, the American continuation of the death penalty could be viewed within the wider moral community of which we are a part as being out of sync with the evolving standard. Even the American who supports the death penalty has evolved morally beyond the view that found the execution of Daniell Frank for stealing a calf acceptable, or the Hebrew Scriptures view that cursing a parent merited death, or the Muslim view, found in the Qu'ran [Muslim holy book], that imposes for the crime of armed robbery death by sword or crucifixion or a cutting off of foot and opposite hand.

China considers opposition to the government just cause for execution. As Americans have leveled human rights abuse charges at China and debated the propriety of extending to China most-favored-nation trading partner status, it is clear that Americans in general find this assertion of just cause for legalized execution inadequate, reflecting a morally deficient barbarism. But if just cause is to be determined relativistically and not morally, China's use of the death penalty is morally wrong only in light of American standards. By the same token, America's use of the death penalty is deficient in light of the move in the wider moral community to abolish the death penalty. Viewed in the context of democratic societies around the world, our retention of the death penalty is as aberrant as the execution of Daniell Frank in Colonial America appears to us today.

One could reply that just cause is established by only one crime, murder, thus making the move Kant made. But this is to mandate capital punishment in the face of the moral presumption against capital punishment that I have taken pains to articulate. By opting for a theory of just execution, we are necessarily excluding—by definition—any absolutist move, including the Kantian move that would support on principle a mandatory use of the death penalty for certain crimes whenever they are committed. If I am right in claiming that we have put just execution into practice in contemporary American society—a point I shall address below—that would mean that many crimes that could fit the description of that crime for which Kant required the death penalty do not, in fact, receive the death penalty, because a morally moderate position will exclude a mandatory death penalty. (Even the [U.S.] Supreme Court, which has upheld the death penalty, refuses to endorse mandatory death sentences.)

If we deny that just cause consists in requiring a mandatory sentence of death for the crime of taking another's life, just execution theory requires that we determine which murders are deserving of death, how the ones we single out for execution are distinctive and thus merit death in ways others do not, then go about the business of using discretion in imposing the death penalty. To mandate a death sentence for a particular crime would be to deny all that we mean by a morally moderate just execution ethic, for just execution would then mean nothing other than resolving to impose death for, say, every murder; and we do not do and will not do that. The moral presumption against the death penalty is too strong and withstands such a challenge.

> *The punishment of death, being extreme, cannot demand more than death.*

But the Kantian position has the merit of simplifying just cause by attaching just cause to a particular crime. In holding that this is insufficient and even contradictory to the just execution ethic, I wish to locate just cause in something other than the offense, which may or may not—as it is considered and deliberated on—give rise to a demand for the death penalty. The foundation of just cause that seems most reasonable to me for calling for the death penalty is one Locke advanced and Mill seemed to address, however obliquely: self-defense.

In the idea of self-defense, we have a justification for execution that natural reason can recognize as sufficient for establishing just cause. When self-defense is the foundation of just cause, we would hold that a criminal offender not only harms innocent persons but poses a continuing threat of harm to persons. Against that threat, society, acting on behalf of the welfare of all, has a right to protect itself. In opting for the death penalty, the society is acting to protect persons from the actual and potential harm a criminal offender embodies for society, and the execution is an act of self-defense that ends a threat that can in no other way be ended with certainty. If the criminal justice system fails to impose sentences consistently and severely, and there is no guarantee that an individual criminal offender guilty of terrible crimes will not later be free to subject innocent persons to harm, then execution is justified—and meets the criterion of just cause—on grounds of self-defense. Capital punishment becomes the means not only of punishing such a criminal, but of assuring that the threat posed to society is definitively removed.

The strongest case for establishing just cause consists not in arguing that murder is the only crime worthy of the death penalty. That is certainly a case to be made and it has merit, but it is not without problems, especially for a theory of just execution that will honor the moral presumption against capital punishment and refuse to insist that capital punishment be imposed for the crime of murder. The strongest case for just cause rests in a self-defense claim. In cases where the threat to the common good is enormous because of the nature of the offender's crime, and there is no way short of execution to ensure that the threat posed by the offender is eradicated, the just execution theorist can appeal to self-defense. When this claim is made and justified, the execution of a criminal offender for reasons of society's self-defense would satisfy the criterion of just cause.

Justice, not vengeance, as motivation

A just execution theory will require that the motivation for an execution be justice and not vengeance. That is not to say that those who survive in the wake of a capital criminal's offense should be expected not to want revenge. The loss of a loved one to murder is a moral horror that only the deepest passion can fathom and for which a desire for retribution is natural. But in the commonwealth of society, as Locke reminded us, "men being partial to themselves, Passion and Revenge is very apt to carry them too far, and with too much heat in their own Cases."

This criterion serves to remind us that the natural desire to harm those who have wronged us must be checked. While retribution seems to be one legitimate motive for punishment, the agent of retribution must never become an individual acting out of a desire for revenge but the collective of society itself, acting through its legal system to dispense justice in accordance with a rule of equal protection and "due process of law." Private vengeance, which would issue from an unchecked desire for revenge, threatens the well-being of all, for we are not, as Locke said, likely to be good or fair judges where our own feelings and interests are concerned, especially when we have been greatly aggrieved. Were the motive of revenge sufficient to justify a killing, that motive would have to be recognized as justifying any and all killings springing from the same motive. This would surely undo any hope of dispensing justice dispassionately or even fairly, since passion might, in the heat of the moment, jump to conclusions and exact vengeance on the wrong party. Kant considered even the desire for vengeance "vicious," but we can acknowledge that desire here as an understandable response by victims of terrible crime or their survivors.

But vengeance is not justice. If what vengeance is seeking is to put right the balance of justice when a capital crime has been committed, we must recognize that vengeance is blind to the irreplaceable nature of the loss suffered. The fact is that the wrongful injury of death is so severe that it cannot be put right. Vengeance can seek justice, but justice is not to be had. Vengeance only serves the illusion that the loss resulting from death can be put right by the death of another. Such a view is folly, sad folly. An irreplaceable loss cannot be replaced; an irretrievable loss cannot be retrieved. And ideally, it is the replacing of the irreplaceable and the retrieving of the irretrievable that justice would require.

We cannot have perfect justice, just execution theory would say—and we ought not have an illusory justice based on vengeance. The best that can be hoped for is dispassionate justice and fair legal adjudication. Dispassionate justice, rather than serving vengeance, might well impose a retributive punishment, but in doing so it would be motivated by justice and not revenge. Such justice, even if clearly retributive, would seek to protect persons from the immoral acts that can spring from vengeance.

Fair imposition

According to this criterion, imposing a death sentence ought not to be based on considerations of race, religion, class, sex, or other accidental features not relevant to establishing that a particular crime is "gravest of the grave" and thus eligible for death penalty consideration. Fairness in just execution theory is not reducible to a Kantian equality principle where the nature of the crime mandates a death sentence. Fairness requires making a determination that capital punishment is a just response to a certain kind of crime, and establishing fairness is accomplished by assessing the crime in light of all kinds of relevant factors. The fairness question is whether imposing the death sentence is fair and just in one case and not another, that determination being affected by mitigating and aggravating circumstances. The law allows consideration of such factors in the penalty phases of capital trials, so that a conviction does not lead inevitably to execution but to an assessment of those factors that have a mitigating effect on punishment, or, conversely, those factors that so aggravate the severity of the crime that the crime is pushed into the category of "gravest of the grave" where death sentences are imposed as proportionate punishment. The law can mitigate punishment and even prohibit consideration of the death penalty for reasons of age and mental ability. Children under sixteen are currently exempt from execution, although this has not always been the case, and mental status is relevant: Arkansas, for instance, prohibits the execution of defendants with IQs below 65. Such persons are held to be not fully responsible for their crimes. It is worth noting that a de facto mitigation of the death penalty occurs in the application of the death penalty relative to class and gender, though pointing out how this occurs provokes fairness questions rather than satisfying the criterion.

> *Deciding on capital punishment must in this sense be a last resort.*

The point of the criterion, however, is to require fairness in the imposition of the death penalty because justice demands it. The standard of fairness is brought to bear to determine the appropriateness of the death penalty in particular cases on the assumption that how such determinations are made can be and ought to be affected by factors that have bearing on the attribution of full responsibility for committing a capital crime. Conviction even in a death penalty–eligible case does not necessitate imposing the death penalty. Even upon conviction in a capital case, a defendant has the opportunity to demonstrate how mitigating factors in his or her particular case ought to prevent the moral presumption against capital punishment from being lifted. Consideration of such factors squares with an ideal of fairness in the imposition of the death penalty.

For all the discrimination that goes on in assessing whether a particular defendant merits mitigation of the death sentence, any discrimination that would affect an impartial distribution of justice would, under this criterion, be disallowed. Disallowed discrimination under this criterion would include considerations of race, religion, class, gender, or any factor incidental to evaluating a case that would regard one person as in some sense more or less valuable than another. This criterion of impartial justice requires that the person who confronts a death sentence do so as a person, a fully endowed member of the moral community, who is neither more nor less deserving of a death sentence than anyone else in a similar situation.

And as a last point, the standard of fairness avowed by this criterion of just execution requires procedural impartiality in the system of justice administration. This aspect of the criterion is potentially troublesome in that fairness that conforms with the moral requirements of justice will require something more than formal observance of a general rule, such as "All persons accused of a capital crime ought to have competent legal representation." The fair imposition criterion is violated if wealth and class can affect the dispensation of justice such that the more resources one has the better chance one has to secure legal representation that will in turn increase the likelihood of evading a death sentence. This is a gray area where disputes will inevitably arise, but just execution demands a moral assessment of those particulars beyond formal observance of a legal rule.

Prohibition on cruelty

This criterion holds that the humanity of persons condemned to death must be respected so that the punishment of death, being extreme, cannot demand more than death. Torture of a condemned person is thus disallowed. Furthermore, the method of execution must be such that it delivers the person to death with dispatch. The force of this criterion is such that it leads to the development of increasingly humane methods of execution. Once-common methods of execution such as boiling in oil, drawing and quartering, garroting, and crucifixion all fail to meet the humaneness standard imposed by this criterion, for these methods involve torture and abuse of the condemned. A botched execution is, in my view, inherently cruel, and although a botched execution is no legal impediment to continuing with the execution, I would argue that morally speaking, an executioner's failure to dispatch an individual in such a way as to eliminate torture renders execution impermissible for this individual, whose sentence of death must then be commuted.

That executions should be humane is certainly not controversial, but the implication of holding firm to this criterion is serious indeed, particularly for those who want to argue that the true foundation of just cause for capital punishment is deterrence. By making execution methods more humane, and then carrying them out in secret, we practically eliminate any justification for the death penalty based on deterrence, at least if deterrence is grounded in Mill's idea that psychological arousal ought to provoke shock and horror at the prospect of execution so that others are deterred from committing capital crimes. Just execution theory would not, to be sure, rest its case on deterrence, and this criterion, if accepted as a legitimate aspect of a just execution theory, in a practical sense, eliminates that possibility.

Last resort

The willful destruction of human life is presumptively wrong, and capital punishment ought not to be a live option unless the decision to use the punishment comes at the end of a long reasoning process that concludes there is no alternative other than demanding forfeiture of life that will satisfy the demands of justice. The presumption against capital punishment is strong and abiding, and it is not to be waived except after thorough deliberation and exhaustive consideration of alternative punishments. Those alternatives must be found wanting. Deciding on capital punishment must in this sense be a last resort, with all other alternatives to execution having been found deficient in delivering proportional justice to the defendant.

Preserving values

This criterion is clearly consequentialist in its focus, and the consequence it points to is this: capital punishment ought not to contribute to a subverting of the value of the good of life in the moral community. This criterion insists that capital punishment be justified by attending to the positive contribution capital punishment makes to advancing and enhancing the value of life. If using this punishment does not make such a contribution but can be shown to subvert the moral community's valuing of the good of life, capital punishment would be deemed morally impermissible.

> *Proportionality requires that the punishment fit the crime.*

This is a troubling criterion because it posits a contradiction. The contradiction is obvious enough: capital punishment ought to enhance and advance the value of life, yet inflicting the death penalty constitutes a killing and is therefore a direct and willful societal assault on the value of life. The contradiction can dissolve if it can be successfully argued that in the name of justice capital punishment assaults the value of a particular life, not the value of life in general; and that by acting to effect the forfeiture of this particular life, society—the moral community—acts to enhance rather than diminish or subvert the value of life. A just execution theory cannot be justified except by such a rationale, and the staunchest and most consistent defenders of capital punishment will make this case. One such defender of capital punishment, Senator Orrin Hatch of Utah, has recognized the importance of this criterion of just execution by stating, "Capital punishment is our society's recognition of the sanctity of human life." Although just execution theory would deny that life is to be valued in accordance with a "sanctity of life" claim, for that would attach absolute value to the value of life and thus deny the foundational premises of just execution as nonabsolute, Hatch's statement does attach capital punishment to the preservation and advancement of the value of life in the moral community. Defending capital punishment on the argument that capital punishment enhances the value of the good of life is, in my view, a necessary move in any just execution theory effort to lift the moral presumption against capital punishment.

This criterion ought to direct our attention back to our moral presumption against killing and the particular destruction of the good of life at issue in capital punishment. For this criterion requires that the integrity of the moral presumption against capital punishment be preserved, even if the criteria of just execution theory have been satisfied and the presumption is justifiably lifted. The effect of an execution ought to be to enhance the good of life and not subvert it. The consequence of capital punishment ought to be that by such action we promote the value of life and thus restore the moral presumption against killing persons—even by the state—to its status as a functioning norm to be honored and observed in the moral community. In other words, an execution performed consistently with a just execution theory ought to reinstate the binding power of the moral presumption against capital punishment, and in no way contribute to a slackening of the force of that presumption. Moral presumptions may be lifted, but it is a condition of lifting them justly that the lifting itself contribute to preserving the values at stake in the presumption. Lifting the presumption in certain circumstances must in no way undermine the value of the good of life or subvert it.

The end of restoring a just equilibrium

Another consequentialist-related criterion of capital punishment is related to the hope that the death penalty will restore equilibrium to the upset balance of justice and thus bring peace to the social order and even to the surviving victims of capital crime. Capital crimes, especially aggravated murder, leave many victims in their wake. The direct victim of the crime is of course the subject of greatest loss; and that loss is absolute and irretrievable. But loss is experienced by those who loved the victim. They too lose in an absolute way a friend, a family member, a person whose value in the interconnectedness of a relational world is beyond measure. The pain of such loss can be excruciating. In the demand society makes for just punishment in the face of absolute loss, the intent of punishment must be directed at bringing the upset scales of justice back into balance to [greatest] the extent possible. When criminal wrongdoers are punished, a positive benefit accrues to society in that society sees itself acting consistently with its own professed commitment to protecting the innocent, ensuring freedom, promoting the value of life and liberty, and pursuing justice. Acting vigorously to prosecute crime and deliver justice through the legal and penal system is what society does to address the disruption in the social equilibrium created by acts of criminal wrongdoing. Social harmony cannot exist in the presence of crime or in the ineffective pursuit of justice in response to crime. The vision of a just society is a shared societal vision: where justice is pursued, a society's common values and its bonds of unity are strengthened; so too when injustice is confronted and unjust acts are punished. Capital punishment ought reasonably to effect the end of enhancing and advancing the cause of justice. By so doing, it promotes social harmony, strengthens the society's bonds of unity, and aims at the end of societal peace.

For the victims of crime, a benefit will hopefully issue from witnessing the society as a whole acting through its system of justice administration to address, correct, and punish individual acts of injustice. For the victims of crime to feel that the offense directed at them has been directed at everyone else as well, and that the power of the collective will be directed toward responding consistently with its professed commitment to justice, reinforces the bonds of social interconnectedness, allowing them to experience the hope that in society's pursuit of justice, peace may be restored in their own lives as individual victims. This is of course a hope. For those who are affected by the irreparable harm of murder, this hope is not easily realized. But delivering justice is always a move in the direction of peace toward the end of peace. And no punishment—including capital punishment—that does not aim at such a restoration of peace should be considered a just punishment.

Capital punishment, in other words, must aim at restoring peace to the surviving victims of capital crime and do so in a way no other punishment can accomplish. That is the message and the requirement of this criterion, and this worthy end—peace—is a necessary feature of any theory of just execution.

Proportionality

This is perhaps the most important criterion in a theory of just execution, but it arises in at least three different ways. First, proportionality requires that the punishment fit the crime. This criterion thus invokes a hierarchy of moral evil and restricts capital punishment to only the gravest crimes, aggravated murder being the most obvious candidate for the death penalty in the serious crime category of homicide.

In accordance with proportionality, capital punishment must, second, not yield an effect disproportionate to the end being sought, whether that end be delivering a just punishment or restoring equilibrium and peace to society and to surviving victims of capital crime.

And third, proportionality requires that capital punishment not violate a person's inherent dignity, whatever that person may have done, however heinous his or her crimes may be. Denying an individual's humanity and refusing to accord the respect he or she is owed by virtue of membership in the moral community constitutes action disproportionate to the crime. As Kant said—and on this point he was clearly right—only persons can be punished. Only fully endowed members of the moral community are capable of assuming responsibility for their actions. Only persons can be held morally accountable by the moral community for acts of wrongdoing. Adding torture or treating a capital criminal in a way that does not accord basic respect to his or her fundamental humanity violates the proportionality criterion and in turn would deny capital punishment justification.

These nine criteria establish the conditions that would have to be met if the presumption against capital punishment is to be justifiably lifted. A theory of just execution would require that all of these criteria be satisfied, and failure to meet them— any one of them—leaves the moral presumption against capital punishment securely in place, functioning as an operative action guide that prevents the granting of moral justification to a proposed execution.

2

Arguments Against the Death Penalty Are Flawed

Thomas R. Eddlem

Thomas R. Eddlem is the editor of the Hanson Express *in Massachusetts. He is a frequent contributor to* New American *and* Point South *magazines.*

Death penalty abolitionists make misleading arguments by using false logic and emotional appeals. Arguments against capital punishment, ranging from the need to grant mercy to the guilty to the dangers of executing the innocent can be systematically refuted point for point. Supporters of capital punishment thus have strong evidence for their position.

R enewed attacks on the death penalty are likely as the trial of accused Twin Tower bombing accomplice Zacharias Moussaoui proceeds. Federal officials have charged Moussaoui with six crimes, four of which carry a potential death sentence. Amnesty International has already issued an "urgent action alert" to call on the world to condemn this "outdated punishment" in the United States. Therefore, there is no time like the present to review some of the misinformation and faulty reasoning of capital punishment opponents.

Fallacy #1: Racism

"The death penalty is racist. . . . The federal death penalty is used disproportionately against minorities, especially African Americans.

Thomas R. Eddlem, "Ten Anti–Death Penalty Fallacies," *The New American*, vol. 18, June 3, 2002. Copyright © 2002 by American Opinion Publishing Inc. Reproduced by permission.

. . . According to [Justice Department] figures, nearly 80% of inmates on federal death row are Black, Hispanic, or from another minority group." (Campaign to End the Death Penalty)

"The imposition of the death penalty is racially biased: Nearly 90% of persons executed were convicted of killing whites, although people of color make up over half of all homicide victims in the United States." (National Coalition to Abolish the Death Penalty)

"Death row in the U.S. has always held a disproportionately large population of people of color relative to the general population." (ACLU Briefing Paper on the Death Penalty)

Correction: The claim that the death penalty unfairly impacts blacks and minorities is a deliberate fraud. The majority of those executed since 1976 have been white, even though black criminals commit a slim majority of murders, if the death penalty is racist, it is biased against white murderers and not blacks.

According to the U.S. Bureau of Justice Statistics, blacks committed 51.5% of murders between 1976 and 1999, while whites committed 46.5%. Yet even though blacks committed a majority of murders, the Bureau of Justice Statistics reports: "Since the death penalty was reinstated by the Supreme Court in 1976, *white* inmates have made up the majority of those under sentence of death." (Emphasis added.) Whites continued to comprise the majority on death row in the year 2000 (1,990 whites to 1,535 blacks and 68 others). In the year 2000, 49 of the 85 people actually put to death were whites.

> *If DNA evidence can really prove innocence, it can prove guilt as well.*

So how can abolitionists claim that the death penalty unfairly punishes black people and other minorities? The statistics they cite are often technically accurate (though not always), but they don't mean what most people assume they mean. Abolitionists often start by analyzing the race of the *victims* rather than the murderers. Because most murders are intraracial (white murderers mostly kill other whites and most black murderers kill other blacks), imposing the death penalty more frequently on white murderers means that killers of white people will more likely be executed. In essence, abolitionists playing the race card argue that black murder victims are not receiving justice because only the murderers of white people are punished with the death penalty. Death penalty proponents may consider this denying justice to black people.

New "hate crimes" laws are likely to worsen the hypocrisy. A "hate crimes" mentality translates into tougher sentences for interracial "hate crimes." Because white people are killed by black people 2.6 times more frequently than black people are killed by white people, more killers of white people will be susceptible to receiving the death penalty than killers of black people.

Fallacy #2: Cost

"It costs more to execute a person than to keep him or her in prison for life. A 1993 California study argues that each death penalty case costs at least $1.25 million more than a regular murder case and a sentence of life without the possibility of parole." (deathpenalty.org)

Correction: While these figures are dubious at best, this argument deserves no response. Justice isn't up for sale to the lowest bidder.

Fallacy #3: Innocence

"A review of death penalty judgments over a 23-year period found a national error rate of 68%." (ACLU Death Penalty Campaign statement)

"Serious error—error substantially undermining the reliability of capital verdicts—has reached epidemic proportions throughout our death penalty system. More than two out of every three capital judgments reviewed by the courts during the 23-year study period were found to be seriously flawed." ("Broken System: Error Rates in Capital Cases, 1973–1995" by James Liebman et al.)

Correction: The major media reported this highly publicized Columbia University study uncritically when it was first released in 2000. But Reg Brown from the Florida governor's office exploded it: "The 'study' defines 'error' to include any issue requiring further review by a lower court. . . . Using the authors' misleading definition, the 'study' does, however, conclude that 64 Florida post-conviction cases were rife with 'error'—even though none of these Florida cases was ultimately resolved by a 'not guilty' verdict, a pardon or a dismissal of murder charges."

Brown noted that even political overturning of death

penalty cases added to the figure. "The nearly 40 death penalty convictions that were reversed by the California Supreme Court during the tenure of liberal activist Rose Bird are treated as 'error cases' when in fact ideological bias was arguably at work." Paul G. Cassell of the *Wall Street Journal* explained how the 68% figure is deceptive: "After reviewing 23 years of capital sentences, the study's authors (like other researchers) were unable to find a single case in which an innocent person was executed. Thus, the most important error rate—the rate of mistaken executions—is zero."

Fallacy #4: DNA evidence

"Since the U.S. Supreme Court ruled in 1976 that capital punishment is not 'cruel and unusual,' 618 prisoners have been executed across the nation and about 80 have been exonerated. . . . Those disturbing odds beg the question: If the chances of executing an innocent person are so high, should we have capital punishment?" (ABC News.com, March 6, 2000)

Correction: While most of those released from death row have been released for political purposes or for technical reasons unrelated to guilt, it is true that a small number have been released because DNA evidence has proven innocence.

But even though ABC may not agree, its news story reinforces why the release of those on death row argues for, not against, the death penalty: "Widespread use of DNA testing and established standards for defense lawyers will virtually eliminate the argument that the death penalty cannot be fairly applied." If DNA evidence can really prove innocence, it can prove guilt as well and society can be all the more certain that criminals sentenced to death will be guilty. The system as a whole is already working well. Since reinstituting the death penalty in 1976, not one person executed in the United States has been later proven innocent as a result of DNA evidence.

Fallacy #5: "Cruel and unusual"

"The death penalty: Always cruel, always inhuman, always degrading . . . there can be no masking the inherent cruelty of the death penalty." (Amnesty International)

"Capital punishment, the ultimate denial of civil liberties, is a costly, irreversible and barbaric practice, the epitome of cruel and unusual punishment." (ACLU Briefing Paper on the Death Penalty)

Correction: The death penalty is not unusual. All of the nations of the world have had the death penalty on the lawbooks throughout most of their recorded history, and the death penalty remains on the statute books of about half of the nations of the world. The death penalty was on the statute books of all the states of the U.S. when the Constitution was adopted. It is far more unusual to have no death penalty than to have a death penalty.

More importantly, the Founding Fathers who adopted the Bill of Rights banning "cruel and unusual punishment" had no problem with implementing the death penalty.

Fallacy #6: Pro-life consistency

"We see the death penalty as perpetuating a cycle of violence and promoting a sense of vengeance in our culture. As we said in Confronting a Culture of Violence: *'We cannot teach that killing is wrong by killing.'" (U.S. Catholic Conference)*

Correction: If capital punishment teaches that it's permissible to kill, do prison sentences teach that it's permissible to hold someone against his will, and do fines teach that it's permissible to steal? In actuality, this fallacy confuses killing the innocent with punishing the guilty. To punish the guilty via the death penalty is not to condone the shedding of innocent blood. Just the opposite, in fact, since capital punishment sends a strong message that murder and other capital crimes will not be tolerated.

> *Capital punishment sends a strong message that murder and other capital crimes will not be tolerated.*

A related fallacy is that the pro-lifer who defends the right to life of an unborn baby in the mother's womb, but who does not defend the right to life of a convicted murderer on death row, is being morally inconsistent. But there is no inconsistency here: The unborn baby is innocent; the convicted murderer is not. It is the pro-abortion/anti-death penalty liberal who is morally inconsistent, since he supports putting to death only the innocent.

Pro-lifers deceive themselves if they imagine abolishing the death penalty will lead to abolishing abortion or a greater respect for life. To the contrary, nations with the death penalty generally restrict abortion more than nations who have abolished the death penalty. Islamic nations and African nations have the death penalty and also have the most prohibitive abortion laws. By contrast, European nations have abolished the death penalty and have liberal abortion laws. Do pro-lifers really want to follow the example of Europe?

Fallacy #7: The company we keep

"The USA is keeping company with notorious human rights abusers. The vast majority of countries in Western Europe, North America and South America—more than 105 nations worldwide—have abandoned capital punishment. The United States remains in the same company as Iraq, Iran, and China as one of the major advocates and users of capital punishment." (deathpenalty.org)

Correction: The arbitrary use of capital punishment in totalitarian societies argues for ensuring that government never abuses this power; it does not argue against the principle of capital punishment, which, in a free society, is applied justly under the rule of law.

The reference to Europe is misleading. Capital punishment advocates are the ones keeping company with common Europeans, while abolitionists are merely keeping company with their elitist governments. Public opinion remains in favor of the death penalty for the most severe murderers throughout much of Europe, but elitist European governments have eliminated using capital punishment.

Fallacy #8: No deterrence

"Capital punishment does not deter crime. Scientific studies have consistently failed to demonstrate that executions deter people from committing crime." (Death Penalty Focus)

Correction: Death penalty opponents love to assume that the principal purpose for capital punishment is deterrence, possibly realizing it is a perfect straw argument. Tangible proof of deterrence alone is not a valid reason for capital punishment (or any other form of punishment, for that matter), nor is it the main rationale employed by astute death penalty advocates. As Christian writer C.S. Lewis observes, "[deterrence] in itself, would be a very wicked thing to do. On the classical theory of punishment it was of course justified on the ground that the man deserved it. Why, in Heaven's name, am I to be sacrificed to the good of society in this way?—unless, of course, I deserve it." Inflicting a penalty merely to deter—rather than to punish for deeds done—is the very definition of cruelty. A purely deterrent penalty is one where a man is punished—not for something that he did—but for something someone else might do. Lewis explained the logical end of this argument: "If deterrence is all that matters, the execution of an innocent man, provided the public think him guilty, would be fully justified."

Men should be punished for their own crimes and not merely to deter others. That said, the death penalty undoubtedly does deter in some cases. For starters, those executed will no longer be around to commit any more crimes.

Fallacy #9: Christian forgiveness and vengeance

"The death penalty appears to oppose the spirit of the Gospel. In the Sermon on the Mount, Jesus urges us to replace the old law of 'an eye for an eye, a tooth for a tooth' with an attitude of charity, even toward those who would commit evil against us (Mw 5:38–48). When asked for his opinion in the case of the woman convicted of adultery, a crime that carried the penalty of death, he immediately pardoned the offender, while deploring the action, the sin (Jn 8). It is difficult for us to accommodate Jesus' injunction to forgive and love, to reconcile and heal, with the practices of executing criminals." (Statement on Capital Punishment by the Christian Council of Delaware and Maryland's Eastern Shore)

> ❝ *Men should be punished for their own crimes and not merely to deter others.* ❞

"In Leviticus, the Lord commanded 'You shall not take vengeance or bear any grudge against the sons of your own people.' Here the Old Testament anticipated Jesus' teaching: 'You have heard it said, "an eye for an eye and a tooth for a tooth." But I say to you, do not resist one who is evil. But if anyone strikes you on the right cheek, turn to him the other one also.' Paul likewise proclaimed that vengeance is reserved for God and that Christians should feed their

enemies, overcoming evil with good (Rom 12:19–21)." (Christianity Today *4-6-98)*

Correction: Punishment—sometimes called retribution—is the main reason for imposing the death penalty. The so-called "Christian" case against the death penalty can be summed up in one sentence: We cannot punish wrongdoers because punishment is always a form of vengeance.

> *❝ Impersonal punishment is far more likely to be proportionate to the crime. ❞*

A careful reading of the Bible does not back up the idea that punishment is synonymous with vengeance. The proportionate retribution required by the Old Testament generally replaced disproportionate vengeance. The same Old Testament that ordered "an eye for an eye and a tooth for a tooth" also prohibited vengeance. Evidently, the Hebrew scriptures view retribution and vengeance as two separate things.

In the New Testament, Jesus denied trying to overturn the Old Testament law. "Do not imagine that I have come to abolish the Law or the Prophets. I have come not to abolish them, but to complete them." (Matthew 5:17) The apostle Paul told the Romans that revenge and retribution are different things entirely. "Never try to get revenge: leave that, my dear friends, to the retribution. As Scripture says, vengeance is mine—I will pay them back, the Lord promises." But then just a few verses later, Paul notes that "if you do wrong, then you may well be afraid; because it is not for nothing that the symbol of authority is the sword: it is there to serve God, too, as his avenger, to bring retribution to wrongdoers." (Romans 13:4) "Authority" refers to the state, which is empowered to put evildoers to the "sword." Paul asserts that the state's retribution of capital punishment is the retribution of God.

Clearly, the Christian Testament regards retribution by the state as not only different from vengeance, but rather as opposites. Vengeance is always personal and it is only rarely proportional to the offense. The Hebrew standard of justice for "an eye for an eye" replaced the hateful and very personal "head for an eye" standard of vengeance. Retribution is impersonal punishment by the state. And impersonal punishment is far

more likely to be proportionate to the crime meaning that it comes closer to the standard of "eye for an eye."

By forgiving the adulterous woman, Jesus was not making a statement against the death penalty. Jesus' enemies thought they had put Christ into a no-win situation by presenting the adulterous woman to him. If Christ ordered the woman's release, they could discredit Him for opposing the Law of Moses. But if He ordered her put to death, then Christ could be handed over to the Roman authorities for the crime of orchestrating a murder. Either way, His opponents figured, they had Him. Christ, of course, knew the hypocritical aims of His enemies had nothing to do with justice. The absence of the man who had committed adultery with the woman "caught in the very act" must have been glaring. His rebuke to "let he who is without sin cast the first stone" was the perfect reply; it highlighted the hypocrisy. Christ's response was in no way a commentary about the death penalty.

Fallacy #10: No mercy

"Capital punishment is society's final assertion that it will not forgive." (Martin Luther King)

"I _____ killing a man. You take away all he's got, and a _____ character in the movie _____

C _____ ath penalty on these _____ hing rather than spirit _____ Clint Eastwood's char _____ surprisingly common _____ ent. The underlying _____ is all that exists. It su _____ erson would seek to t _____

seel _____ pital punishment not _____ Thomas Aquinas inf _____ be dangerous and pra _____ of some sin, it is saf _____ killed in order to th _____ alty for murderers, fo _____ gian argued, was a isl _____ ed that this "punished _____ ot only healing the pa _____ ." Though life may

be taken from a murderer, he will be better off with the punishment because "spiritual goods are of the greatest consequence, while temporal goods are least important."

Unfortunately, it doesn't seem to dawn on proponents employing this faulty reasoning that perhaps a just punishment in this world would best prepare a criminal for the next.

3

Retribution Is a Moral Reason for Capital Punishment

Walter Berns

Walter Berns, resident scholar of the American Scholar Institute and an international public speaker, writes about constitutional law, legal issues, and political philosophy. His publication For Capital Punishment: Crime and the Morality of the Death Penalty *(1979) appeared just three years after capital punishment was declared constitutional.*

Abolitionists distrust and dismiss retribution as a justification for capital punishment. They do not understand that the anger a community feels toward a criminal who has caused the innocent to suffer is a sign of the highest morality. This kind of anger leads people to seek justice and protect their community. Society is justified in executing serious criminals in order to achieve justice and retribution.

Until recently, my business did not require me to think about the punishment of criminals in general or the legitimacy and efficacy of capital punishment in particular. In a vague way, I was aware of the disagreement among professionals concerning the purpose of punishment—whether it was intended to deter others, to rehabilitate the criminal, or to pay him back—but like most laymen I had no particular reason to decide which purpose was right or to what extent they may all have been right. I did know that retribution was held in ill repute among criminologists and jurists—to them, retribution was a fancy name for revenge, and revenge was barbaric—and, of course, I knew that capital punishment had the support only of policemen, prison guards, and some local politicians, the sort of people [Hungarian philosopher] Arthur Koestler calls "hanghards.". . . The intellectual community denounced it as both unnecessary and immoral. It was the phenomenon of [Holocaust survivor and human rights activist] Simon Wiesenthal that allowed me to understand why the intellectuals were wrong and why the police, the politicians, and the majority of the voters were right: We punish criminals principally in order to pay them back, and we execute the worst of them out of moral necessity. Anyone who respects Wiesenthal's mission will be driven to the same conclusion. . . .

Modern civil-libertarian opponents of capital punishment do not understand this. They say that to execute a criminal is to deny his human dignity; they also say that the death penalty is not useful, that nothing useful is accomplished by executing anyone. Being utilitarians, they are essentially selfish men, distrustful of passion, who do not understand the connection between anger and justice, and between anger and human dignity.

Understanding anger

Anger is expressed or manifested on those occasions when someone has acted in a manner that is thought to be unjust, and one of its origins is the opinion that men are responsible, and should be held responsible, for what they do. Thus, as [Greek philosopher] Aristotle teaches us, anger is accompanied not only by the pain caused by the one who is the object of anger, but by the pleasure arising from the expectation of inflicting revenge on someone who is thought to deserve it. We can become angry with an inanimate object (the door we run into and then kick in return) only by foolishly attributing responsibility to it, and we cannot do that for long, which is why we do not think of returning later to revenge ourselves on the door. For the same reason, we cannot be more than momentarily angry with any one creature other than man; only a fool and worse would dream of taking revenge on a dog. And, finally, we tend to pity rather than to be angry with men who—because they are insane, for example—are not responsible for their acts. Anger, then, is a very human passion not only because only a human being can be angry, but also because anger acknowledges the humanity of its objects: it holds them accountable for what they do. And in holding particular men responsible, it pays them the respect that is due them as men.

Anger recognizes that only men have the capacity to be moral beings and, in so doing, acknowledges the dignity of human beings. Anger is somehow connected with justice, and it is this that modern penology has not understood; it tends on the whole, to regard anger as a selfish indulgence.

Useful anger

Anger can, of course, be that; and if someone does not become angry with an insult or an injury suffered unjustly, we tend to think he does not think much of himself. But it need not be selfish, not in the sense of being provoked only by an injury suffered by oneself. There were many angry men in America when President [John F.] Kennedy was killed; one of them— Jack Ruby[1]—took it upon himself to exact the punishment that, if indeed deserved, ought to have been exacted by the law. There were perhaps even angrier men when [civil rights activist] Martin Luther King Jr. was killed, for King, more than anyone else at the time, embodied a people's quest for justice; the anger—more, the "black rage"—expressed on that occasion was simply a manifestation of the great change that had occurred among black men in America, a change wrought in large part by King and his associates in the civil-rights movement; the servility and fear of the past had been replaced by pride and anger, and the treatment that had formerly been accepted as a matter of course or as if it were deserved was now seen for what it was, unjust and unacceptable. King preached love, but the movement he led depended on anger as well as love, and that anger was not despicable, being neither selfish nor unjustified. On the contrary, it was a reflection of what was called solidarity and may more accurately be called a profound caring for others, black for other blacks, white for blacks, and, in the world King was trying to build, American for other Americans. If men are not saddened when someone else suffers, or angry when someone else suffers unjustly, the implication is that they do not care for anyone other than themselves or that they lack some quality that befits a man. When we criticize them for this, we acknowledge that they ought to care for others. If men are not angry when a neighbor suffers at the hands of a criminal, the implication is that their moral facul-

---

1. Jack Ruby shot Kennedy's assassin, Lee Harvey Oswald.

ties have been corrupted, that they are not good citizens.

Criminals are properly the objects of anger, and the perpe-trators of terrible crimes—for example, [Kennedy's assassin] Lee Harvey Oswald and [King's assassin] James Earl Ray—are prop-erly the objects of great anger. They have done more than in-flict an injury on an isolated individual; they have violated the foundations of trust and friendship, the necessary elements of a moral community, the only community worth living in. A moral community, unlike a hive of bees or a hill of ants, is one whose members are expected freely to obey the laws and, un-like those in a tyranny, are trusted to obey the laws. The crimi-nal has violated that trust, and in so doing has injured not merely his immediate victim but the community as such. He has called into question the very possibility of that community by suggesting that men cannot be trusted to respect freely the property, the person, and the dignity of those with whom they are associated. If, then, men are not angry when someone else is robbed, raped, or murdered, the implication is that no moral community exists, because those men do not care for anyone other than themselves. Anger is an expression of that caring, and society needs men who care for one another, who share their pleasures and their pains, and do so for the sake of the oth-ers. It is the passion that can cause us to act for reasons having nothing to do with selfish or mean calculation; indeed, when educated, it can become a generous passion, the passion that protects the community or country by demanding punishment for its enemies. It is the stuff from which heroes are made. . . .

Divine inspiration

What can a dramatic poet tell us about murder? More, proba-bly, than anyone else, if he is a poet worthy of consideration, and yet nothing that does not inhere in the act itself. In [the play] *Macbeth* [playwright William] Shakespeare shows us mur-ders committed in a political world by a man so driven by am-bition to rule that world that he becomes a tyrant. He shows us also the consequences, which were terrible, worse even than Macbeth[2] feared. The cosmos rebelled, turned into chaos by his deeds. He shows a world that was not "benignly indifferent" to what we call crimes and especially to murder, a world consti-tuted by laws divine as well as human, and Macbeth violated

2. Macbeth murdered the king and usurped the throne.

the most awful of those laws. Because the world was so consti-
tuted, Macbeth suffered the torments of the great and the
damned, torments far beyond the "practice" of any physician.
He had known glory and had deserved the respect and affection of king, countrymen, army, friends, and wife; and he lost
it all. At the end he was reduced to saying that life "is a tale told
by an idiot, full of sound and fury, signifying nothing"; yet, in
spite of the horrors provoked in us by his acts, he excites no
anger in us. We pity him; even so, we understand the anger of
his countrymen and the dramatic necessity of his death. *Macbeth* is a play about ambition, murder, tyranny; about horror,
anger, vengeance, and perhaps more than any other of Shakespeare's plays, justice. Because of justice, Macbeth has to die,
not by his own hand—he will not "play the Roman fool, and
die on [his] sword"—but at the hand of the avenging Macduff
[a noble wronged by Macbeth]. The dramatic necessity of his
death would appear to rest on its moral necessity. Is that right?
Does the play conform to our sense of what a murder means?
[Abraham] Lincoln thought it was "wonderful.". . .

> **"** *Anger is somehow connected with justice.* **"**

Shakespeare shows us vengeful men because there is something in the souls of men—then and now—that requires such
crimes to be avenged. Can we imagine a world that does not take
its revenge on the man who kills Macduff's wife and children?
(Can we imagine the play in which Macbeth does not die?) Can
we imagine a people that does not hate murderers? (Can we
imagine a world where Meursault[3] is an outsider only because he
does not pretend to be outraged by murder?) Shakespeare's poetry could not have been written out of the moral sense that the
death penalty's opponents insist we ought to have. . . .

There is a sense in which punishment may be likened to
dramatic poetry. Dramatic poetry depicts men's actions because men are revealed in, or make themselves known
through, their actions; and the essence of a human action, according to Aristotle, consists in its being virtuous or vicious.

3. Meursault is the central character in Albert Camus' *The Stranger*. He is an indifferent person who kills in self-defense and is convicted of murder because of
irrelevant evidence.

Only a ruler or a contender for a rule can act with the freedom
and on a scale that allows the virtuousness or viciousness of
human deeds to be fully displayed. Macbeth was such a man,
and in his fall, brought about by his own acts, and in the con-
sequent suffering he endured, is revealed the meaning of
morality. In *Macbeth* the majesty of the moral law is demonstrated to us; as I said, it teaches us the awesomeness of the
commandment Thou shalt not kill. In a similar fashion, the
punishments imposed by the legal order remind us of the reign
of the moral order; not only do they remind us of it, but by enforcing its prescriptions, they enhance the dignity of the legal
order in the eyes of moral men, in the eyes of those decent citizens who cry out "for gods who will avenge injustice." That is
especially important in a self-governing community, a community that gives laws to itself.

> *Despite its venerable character, the Constitution is not the only source of these moral sensibilities.*

If the laws were understood to be divinely inspired or, in the
extreme case, divinely given, they would enjoy all the dignity
that the opinions of men can grant and all the dignity they require to ensure their being obeyed by most of the men living
under them. Like Duncan[4] in the opinion of Macduff, the laws
would be "the Lord's anointed," and would be obeyed even as
Macduff obeyed the laws of the Scottish kingdom. Only a Macbeth would challenge them. . . . But the laws of the United
States are not of this description; in fact, among the proposed
amendments that became the Bill of Rights was one declaring,
not that all power comes from God, but rather "that all power
is originally vested in, and consequently derives from the
people"; and this proposal was dropped only because it was
thought to be redundant: the Constitution's preamble said essentially the same thing, and what we know as the Tenth
Amendment reiterated it. So [James] Madison proposed to make
the Constitution venerable in the minds of the people, and Lincoln, in an early speech, went so far as to say that a "political re-

4. the king of Scotland murdered by Macbeth

ligion" should be made of it. They did not doubt that the Constitution and the laws made pursuant to it would be supported by "enlightened reason," but fearing that enlightened reason would be in short supply, they sought to augment it. The laws of the United States would be obeyed by some men because they could hear and understand "the voice of enlightened reason," and by other men because they would regard the laws with that "veneration which time bestows on everything."

Constitutional authority

Supreme Court justices have occasionally complained of our habit of making "constitutionality synonymous with wisdom." But the extent to which the Constitution is venerated and its authority accepted depends on the compatibility of its rules with our moral sensibilities; despite its venerable character, the Constitution is not the only source of these moral sensibilities. There was even a period, before slavery was abolished by the Thirteenth Amendment, when the Constitution was regarded by some very moral men as abomination. [Statesman William Lloyd] Garrison called it "a covenant with death and an agreement with Hell," and there were honorable men holding important political offices and judicial appointments who refused to enforce the Fugitive Slave Law[5] even though its constitutionality had been affirmed. In time this opinion spread far beyond the ranks of the original abolitionists until those who held it composed a constitutional majority of the people, and slavery was abolished.

But Lincoln knew that more than amendments were required to make the Constitution once more [in 1863] worthy of the veneration of moral men. That is why, in the Gettysburg Address, he made the principle of the Constitution an inheritance from "our fathers." That it should be so esteemed is especially important in a self-governing nation that gives laws to itself, because it is only a short step from the principle that the laws are merely a product of one's own will to the opinion that the only consideration that informs the law is self-interest; and this opinion is only one remove from lawlessness. A nation of simply self-interested men will soon enough perish from the earth.

It was not an accident that Lincoln spoke as he did at Gettysburg [Pennsylvania] or that he chose as the occasion for his

5. a law that allowed slave owners to reclaim their runaway slaves

words the dedication of a cemetery built on a portion of the most significant battlefield of the Civil War. Two and a half years earlier, in his first inaugural address, he had said that Americans, north and south, were not and must not be enemies, but friends. Passion had strained but must not be allowed to break the bonds of affection that tied them one to another. He closed by saying this: "The mystic chords of memory, stretching from every battlefield, and patriot grave, to every living heart and hearthstone, all over this broad land, will yet swell the chorus of the Union, when again touched, as surely they will be, by the better angels of our nature." The chords of memory that would swell the chorus of the Union could be touched, even by a man of Lincoln's stature, only on the most solemn occasions, and in the life of a nation no occasion is more solemn than the burial of the patriots who have died defending it on the field of battle. War is surely an evil, but as [German philosopher Georg Wilhelm Friedrich] Hegel said, it is not an "absolute evil." It exacts the supreme sacrifice, but precisely because of that it can call forth such sublime rhetoric as Lincoln's. His words at Gettysburg serve to remind Americans in particular of what Hegel said people in general needed to know, and could be made to know by means of war and the sacrifices demanded of them in wars: namely, that their country is something more than a "civil society" the purpose of which is simply the protection of individual and selfish interests.

Dignity and the ultimate penalty

Capital punishment, like Shakespeare's dramatic and Lincoln's political poetry (and it is surely that, and was understood by him to be that), serves to remind us of the majesty of the moral order that is embodied in our law, and of the terrible consequences of its breach. The law must not be understood to be merely a statute that we enact or repeal at our will, and obey or disobey at our convenience—especially not the criminal law. Wherever law is regarded as merely statutory, men will soon enough disobey it, and will learn how to do so without any inconvenience to themselves. The criminal law must possess a dignity far beyond that possessed by mere statutory enactment or utilitarian and self-interested calculations. The most powerful means we have to give it that dignity is to authorize it to impose the ultimate penalty. The criminal law must be made awful, by which I mean inspiring, or commanding "profound respect or reverential fear." It must remind us of the moral order by which alone we can live as human beings, and in America, now that the Supreme Court has outlawed banishment, the only punishment that can do this is capital punishment.

> *Punishment arises out of the demand for justice, and justice is demanded by angry, morally indignant men.*

The founder of modern criminology, the eighteenth-century Italian Cesare Beccaria, opposed both banishment and capital punishment because he understood that both were inconsistent with the principle of self-interest, and self-interest was the basis of the political order he favored. If a man's first or only duty is to himself, of course he will prefer his money to his country, he will also prefer his money to his brother. In fact, he will prefer his brother's money to his brother, and a people of this description, or a country that understands itself in this Beccarian manner, can put the mark of Cain[6] on no one. For the same reason, such a country can have no legitimate reason to execute its criminals, or, indeed, to punish them in any manner. What would be accomplished by punishment in such a place? Punishment arises out of the demand for justice, and justice is demanded by angry, morally indignant men; its purpose is to satisfy that moral indignation and thereby promote the law-abidingness that, it is assumed, accompanies it. But the principle of self-interest denies the moral basis of that indignation.

Not only will a country based solely on self-interest have no legitimate reason to punish; it may have no need to punish. . . .

When, in 1976, the Supreme Court declared death to be a constitutional penalty, it decided that the United States was not [a country based on self-interest]; most of us, I think, can appreciate that judgment. We want to live among people who do not value their possessions more than their citizenship, who do not think exclusively or even primarily of their own rights, people whom we can depend on even as they exercise their rights, and whom we can trust, which is to say, people who, even in the absence of a policeman, will not assault our bodies

6. in the biblical story, the mark placed on Cain for committing murder

or steal our possessions, and might even come to our assistance when we need it, and who stand ready, when the occasion demands it, to risk their lives in defense of their country. If we are of the opinion that the United States may rightly ask of its citizens this awful sacrifice, then we are also of the opinion that it may rightly impose the most awful penalty; if it may rightly honor its heroes, it may rightly execute the worst of its criminals. By doing so, it will remind its citizens that it is a country worthy of heroes.

4

The Possibility That the Death Penalty Deters Murder Justifies Its Use

Ernest van den Haag

Until his death in March 2002, Ernest van den Haag was a nationally known Heritage Foundation scholar and regular contributing editor to the National Review. *He was also the author of many books and articles on the death penalty, including his frequently cited article "The Ultimate Punishment: A Defense" (1986), in which he refutes the most popular arguments for the abolition of the death penalty. His books include* The Death Penalty: A Debate *(1983),* Is Capital Punishment Just? *(1978), and* Punishing Criminals: Concerning a Very Old and Painful Question *(1975).*

A common argument in favor of capital punishment is that it deters potential criminals. Although there is no statistical proof that the death penalty deters crime, it is a fair and logical assumption that it could. Even irrational and self-destructive criminals may be deterred by the threat of capital punishment, thus preventing the murder of innocent people. Although some argue that capital punishment is wrong because innocent people could be wrongly convicted and executed, that risk is outweighed by the number of people who potentially will be saved from criminals deterred by capital punishment.

If rehabilitation and the protection of society from unrehabilitated offenders were the only purposes of legal punishment the death penalty could be abolished: It cannot attain the first end, and is not needed for the second. No case for the death penalty can be made unless "doing justice," or "deterring others," are among our penal aims. Each of these purposes can justify capital punishment by itself; opponents, therefore, must show that neither actually does, while proponents can rest their case on either. . . .

Justice, innocents, and capital punishment

Capital punishment is regarded as unjust because it may lead to the execution of innocents, or because the guilty poor (or disadvantaged) are more likely to be executed than the guilty rich.

Regardless of merit, these claims are relevant only if "doing justice" is one purpose of punishment. Unless one regards it as good, or, at least, better, that the guilty be punished rather than the innocent, and that the equally guilty be punished equally, unless, that is, one wants penalties to be just, one cannot object to them because they are not. However, if one does include justice among the purposes of punishment, it becomes possible to justify any one punishment—even death—on grounds of justice. Yet, those who object to the death penalty because of its alleged injustice, usually deny not only the merits, or the sufficiency, of specific arguments based on justice, but the propriety of justice as an argument: They exclude "doing justice" as a purpose of legal punishment. If justice is not a purpose of penalties, injustice cannot be an objection to the death penalty, or to any other; if it is, justice cannot be ruled out as an argument for any penalty.

> *It is not the penalty—whether death or prison—which is unjust when inflicted on the innocent, but its imposition on the innocent.*

Consider the claim of injustice on its merits now. A convicted man may be found to have been innocent; if he was executed, the penalty cannot be reversed. Except for fines, penalties never can be reversed. Time spent in prison cannot be returned. However, a prison sentence may be remitted once the prisoner serving it is found innocent; and he can be compensated for the time served (although compensation ordinarily cannot repair the harm). Thus, though (nearly) all penalties are irreversible, the death penalty, unlike others, is irrevocable as well.

Despite all precautions, errors will occur in judicial proceedings: The innocent may be found guilty, or the guilty rich may more easily escape conviction, or receive lesser penalties than the guilty poor. However, these injustices do not reside in the penalties inflicted but in their maldistribution. It is not the penalty—whether death or prison—which is unjust when inflicted on the innocent, but its imposition on the innocent. Inequity between poor and rich also involves distribution, not the penalty distributed. Thus injustice is not an objection to the death penalty but to the distributive process—the trial. Trials are more likely to be fair when life is at stake—the death penalty is probably less often unjustly inflicted than others. It requires special consideration not because it is more, or more often, unjust than other penalties, but because it is always irrevocable.

Does any punishment 'deter others' at all?

Can any amount of deterrence justify the possibility of irrevocable injustice? Surely injustice is unjustifiable in each actual individual case; it must be objected to whenever it occurs. But we are concerned here with the process that may produce injustice, and with the penalty that would make it irrevocable—not with the actual individual cases produced, but with the general rules which may produce them. To consider objections to a general rule (the provision of any penalties by law) we must compare the likely net result of alternative rules and select the rule (or penalty) likely to produce the least injustice. For however one defines justice, to support it cannot mean less than to favor the least injustice. If the death of innocents because of judicial error is unjust, so is the death of innocents by murder. If some murders could be avoided by a penalty conceivably more deterrent than others—such as the death penalty—then the question becomes: Which penalty will minimize the number of innocents killed (by crime and by punishment)? It follows that the irrevocable injustice sometimes inflicted by the death penalty would not significantly militate against it, if capital punishment deters enough murders to reduce the total number of innocents killed so that fewer are lost than would be lost without it. . . .

Deterrence depends on response to danger

Does any punishment "deter others" at all? Doubts have been thrown on this effect because it is thought to depend on the incorrect rationalistic psychology of some of its eighteenth- and nineteenth-century proponents. Actually deterrence does not depend on rational calculation, on rationality or even on capacity for it; nor do arguments for it depend on rationalistic psychology. Deterrence depends on the likelihood and on the regularity—not on the rationality—of human responses to danger; and further on the possibility of reinforcing internal controls by vicarious external experiences.

Responsiveness to danger is generally found in human behavior; the danger can, but need not, come from the law or from society; nor need it be explicitly verbalized. Unless intent on suicide, people do not jump from high mountain cliffs, however tempted to fly through the air; and they take precautions against falling. The mere risk of injury often restrains us from doing what is otherwise attractive; we refrain even when we have no direct experience, and usually without explicit computation of probabilities, let alone conscious weighing of expected pleasure against possible pain. One abstains from dangerous acts because of vague, inchoate, habitual and, above all, preconscious fears. Risks and rewards are more often felt than calculated; one abstains without accounting to oneself, because "it isn't done," or because one literally does not conceive of the action one refrains from. Animals as well refrain from painful or injurious experiences presumably without calculation; and the threat of punishment can be used to regulate their conduct.

Unlike natural dangers, legal threats are constructed deliberately by legislators to restrain actions which may impair the social order. Thus legislation transforms social into individual dangers. Most people further transform external into internal danger: They acquire a sense of moral obligation, a conscience, which threatens them, should they do what is wrong. Arising originally from the external authority of rulers and rules, conscience is internalized and becomes independent of external forces. However, conscience is constantly reinforced in those whom it controls by the coercive imposition of external authority on recalcitrants and on those who have not acquired it. Most people refrain from offenses because they feel an obligation to behave lawfully. But this obligation would scarcely be felt if those who do not feel or follow it were not to suffer punishment. . . .

To be sure, not everybody responds to threatened punishment. Nonresponsive persons may be (a) self-destructive or (b) incapable of responding to threats, or even of grasping them. Increases in the size, or certainty, of penalties would not affect these two groups. A third group (c) might respond to more certain or more severe penalties. If the punishment threatened for burglary, robbery, or rape were a $5 fine in North Carolina, and five years in prison in South Carolina, I have no doubt that the North Carolina treasury would become quite opulent until vigilante justice would provide the deterrence not provided by law. Whether to increase penalties (or improve enforcement) depends on the importance of the rule to society, the size and likely reaction of the group that did not respond before, and the acceptance of the added punishment and enforcement required to deter it. Observation would have to locate the points—likely to differ in different times and places—at which diminishing, zero, and negative returns set in. There is no reason to believe that all present and future offenders belong to the *a priori* nonresponsive groups, or that all penalties have reached the point of diminishing, let alone zero returns.

Debate over the causes of crime

Even though its effectiveness seems obvious, punishment as a deterrent has fallen into disrepute. Some ideas which help explain this progressive heedlessness were uttered by Lester Pearson, then Prime Minister of Canada, when, in opposing the death penalty, he proposed that instead "the state seek to eradicate the causes of crime—slums, ghettos and personality disorders."

"Slums, ghettos and personality disorders" have not been shown; singly or collectively, to be "the causes" of crime.

(1) The crime rate in the slums is indeed higher than elsewhere; but so is the death rate in hospitals. Slums are no more "causes" of crime, than hospitals are of death; they are locations of crime, as hospitals are of death. Slums and hospitals attract people selectively; neither is the "cause" of the condition (disease in hospitals, poverty in slums) that leads to the selective attraction.

As for poverty which draws people into slums, and, sometimes, into crime, any relative disadvantage may lead to ambition, frustration, resentment and, if insufficiently restrained, to crime. Not all relative disadvantages can be eliminated; indeed very few can be, and their elimination increases the resentment generated by the remaining ones; not even relative poverty can be removed altogether. (Absolute poverty—whatever that may be—hardly affects crime.) However, though contributory, relative disadvantages are not a necessary or sufficient cause of crime: Most poor people do not commit crimes, and some rich people do. Hence, "eradication of poverty" would, at most, remove one (doubtful) cause of crime. . . .

> *The question is not only whether the penalty deters, but whether it deters more than alternatives and whether the difference exceeds the cost of irrevocability.*

Those who regard poverty as a cause of crime often draw a wrong inference from a true proposition: The rich will not commit certain crimes—[indusrialist and business magnate John D.] Rockefeller never riots; nor does he steal. . . . Yet while wealth may be the cause of not committing (certain) crimes, it does not follow that poverty (absence of wealth) is the cause of committing them. Water extinguishes or prevents fire; but its absence is not the cause of fire. Thus, if poverty could be abolished, if everybody had all "necessities" (I don't pretend to know what this would mean), crime would remain, for, in the words of [Greek philosopher] Aristotle, "the greatest crimes are committed not for the sake of basic necessities but for the sake of superfluities." Superfluities cannot be provided by the government; they would be what the government does not provide.

(2) . . . Ethnic separation, voluntary or forced, obviously has little to do with crime; I can think of no reason why it should.

(3) I cannot see how the state could "eradicate" personality disorders even if all causes and cures were known and available. (They are not.) Further, the known incidence of personality disorders within the prison population does not exceed the known incidence outside—though our knowledge of both is tenuous. Nor are personality disorders necessary, or sufficient causes for criminal offenses, unless these be identified by means of (moral, not clinical) definition with personality disorders. In this case, Mr. Pearson would have proposed to "eradicate" crime by eradicating crime—certainly a sound, but not a helpful idea.

Mr. Pearson's views are part as well of the mental furniture of the former U.S. Attorney General Ramsey Clark, who told a congressional committee that ". . . only the elimination of the causes of crime can make a significant and lasting difference in the incidence of crime." Uncharitably interpreted, Mr. Clark revealed that only the elimination of causes eliminates effects—a sleazy cliché and wrong to boot. Given the benefit of the doubt, Mr. Clark probably meant that the causes of crime are social; and that therefore crime can be reduced "only" by non-penal (social) measures.

This view suggests a fireman who declines fire-fighting apparatus by pointing out that "in the long run only the elimination of the causes" of fire "can make a significant and lasting difference in the incidence" of fire, and that fire-fighting equipment does not eliminate "the causes"—except that such a fireman would probably not rise to fire chief. Actually, whether fires are checked, depends on equipment and on the efforts of the firemen using it no less than on the presence of "the causes": inflammable materials. So with crimes. Laws, courts, and police actions are no less important in restraining them than "the causes" are in impelling them. If firemen (or attorneys general) pass the buck and refuse to use the means available, we may all be burned while waiting for "the long run" and the "elimination of the causes.". . .

Does the death penalty deter criminals?

The foregoing suggests the question posed by the death penalty: Is the deterrence added sufficiently above zero to warrant irrevocability (or other, less clear, disadvantages)? The question is not only whether the penalty deters, but whether it deters more than alternatives and whether the difference exceeds the cost of irrevocability. (I shall assume that the alternative is actual life imprisonment so as to exclude the complication produced by the release of the unrehabilitated.)

In some fairly infrequent but important circumstances the death penalty is the only possible deterrent. Thus, in case of acute *coups d'état*, or of acute substantial attempts to overthrow the government, prospective rebels would altogether discount the threat of any prison sentence. They would not be deterred because they believe the swift victory of the revolution will invalidate a prison sentence and turn it into an advantage. Execution would be the only deterrent because, unlike prison sentences, it cannot be revoked by victorious rebels. The same reasoning applies to deterring spies or traitors in wartime. Finally, men who, by virtue of past acts, are already serving, or are threatened, by a life sentence, could be deterred from further offenses only by the threat of the death penalty.

What about criminals who do not fall into any of these (often ignored) classes? Professor [of sociology] Thorsten Sellin has made a careful study of the available statistics: He concluded that they do not yield evidence for the deterring effect of the death penalty. Somewhat surprisingly, Professor Sellin seems to think that this lack of evidence for deterrence is evidence for the lack of deterrence. It is not. It means that deterrence has not been demonstrated statistically—not that nondeterrence has been.

It is entirely possible, indeed likely (as Professor Sellin appears willing to concede), that the statistics used, though the best available, are nonetheless too slender a reed to rest conclusions on. They indicate that the homicide rate does not vary greatly between similar areas with or without the death penalty, and in the same area before and after abolition. However, the similar areas are not similar enough; the periods are not long enough; many social differences and changes, other than the abolition of the death penalty, may account for the variation (or lack of) in homicide rates with and without, before and after abolition; some of these social differences and changes are likely to have affected homicide rates. I am unaware of any statistical analysis which adjusts for such changes and differences. And logically, it is quite consistent with the postulated deterrent effect of capital punishment that there be less homicide after abolition: With retention there might have been still less.

Homicide rates do not depend exclusively on penalties any more than do other crime rates. A number of conditions which influence the propensity to crime, demographic, economic or generally social changes or differences—even such matters as changes of the divorce laws or of the cotton price—may influence the homicide rate. Therefore, variation or constancy cannot be attributed to variations or constancy of the penalties, unless we know that no other factor influencing the homicide rate has changed. Usually we don't. To believe the death penalty deterrent does not require one to believe that the death penalty, or any other, is the only, or the decisive, causal variable; this would be as absurd as the converse mistake that "social causes" are the only, or always, the decisive factor. To favor capital punishment, the efficacy of neither variable need be denied. It is enough to affirm that the severity of the penalty may influence some potential criminals, and that the added severity of the death penalty adds to deterrence, or may do so. It is quite possible that such a deterrent effect may be offset (or intensified) by nonpenal factors which affect propensity; its presence or absence therefore may be hard, and perhaps impossible to demonstrate.

Contrary to what Professor Sellin et al. seem to presume, I doubt that offenders are aware of the absence or presence of the death penalty state by state or period by period. Such unawareness argues against the assumption of a calculating murderer. However, unawareness does not argue against the death penalty if by deterrence we mean a preconscious, general response to a severe, but not necessarily specifically and explicitly apprehended, or calculated threat. A constant homicide rate, despite abolition, may occur because of unawareness and not because of lack of deterrence: People remain deterred for a lengthy interval by the severity of the penalty in the past, or by the severity of penalties used in similar circumstances nearby.

> *I believe we have no right to risk additional future victims of murder for the sake of sparing convicted murderers.*

I do not argue for a version of deterrence which would require me to believe that an individual shuns murder while in North Dakota, because of the death penalty, and merrily goes to it in South Dakota since it has been abolished there; or that he will start the murderous career from which he had hitherto refrained, after abolition. I hold that the generalized threat of the death penalty may be a deterrent, and the more so, the more generally applied. Deterrence will not cease in the particular areas of abolition or at the particular times of abolition. Rather, general deterrence will be somewhat weakened, through local (partial) abolition. Even such weakening will be hard to detect owing to changes in many offsetting, or reinforcing, factors.

For all of these reasons, I doubt that the presence or absence of a deterrent effect of the death penalty is likely to be demonstrable by statistical means. The statistics presented by

Professor Sellin et al. show only that there is no statistical proof for the deterrent effect of the death penalty. But they do not show that there is no deterrent effect. Not to demonstrate presence of the effect is not the same as to demonstrate its absence; certainly not when there are plausible explanations for the nondemonstrability of the effect.

It is on our uncertainty that the case for deterrence must rest.

Accept uncertainty

If we do not know whether the death penalty will deter others, we are confronted with two uncertainties. If we impose the death penalty, and achieve no deterrent effect thereby, the life of a convicted murderer has been expended in vain (from a deterrent viewpoint). There is a net loss. If we impose the death sentence and thereby deter some future murderers, we spared the lives of some future victims (the prospective murderers gain, too; they are spared punishment because they were deterred). In this case, the death penalty has led to a net gain, unless the life of a convicted murderer is valued more highly than that of the unknown victim, or victims (and the nonimprisonment of the deterred nonmurderer).

The calculation can be turned around, of course. The absence of the death penalty may harm no one and therefore produce a gain—the life of the convicted murderer. Or it may kill future victims of murderers who could have been deterred, and thus produce a loss—their life.

To be sure, we must risk something certain—the death (or life) of the convicted man, for something uncertain—the death (or life) of the victims of murderers who may be deterred. This is in the nature of uncertainty—when we invest, or gamble, we risk the money we have for an uncertain gain. Many human actions, most commitments—including marriage and crime—share this characteristic with the deterrent purpose of any penalization, and with its rehabilitative purpose (and even with the protective).

More proof is demanded for the deterrent effect of the death penalty than is demanded for the deterrent effect of other penalties. This is not justified by the absence of other utilitarian purposes such as protection and rehabilitation; they involve no less uncertainty than deterrence.

Irrevocability may support a demand for some reason to expect more deterrence than revocable penalties might produce, but not a demand for more proof of deterrence, as has been pointed out above. The reason for expecting more deterrence lies in the greater severity, the terrifying effect inherent in finality. Since it seems more important to spare victims than to spare murderers, the burden of proving that the greater severity inherent in irrevocability adds nothing to deterrence lies on those who oppose capital punishment. Proponents of the death penalty need show only that there is no more uncertainty about it than about greater severity in general.

The demand that the death penalty be proved more deterrent than alternatives cannot be satisfied any more than the demand that six years in prison be proved to be more deterrent than three. But the uncertainty which confronts us favors the death penalty as long as by imposing it we might save future victims of murder. This effect is as plausible as the general idea that penalties have deterrent effects which increase with their severity. Though we have no proof of the positive deterrence of the penalty, we also have no proof of zero, or negative effectiveness. I believe we have no right to risk additional future victims of murder for the sake of sparing convicted murderers; on the contrary, our moral obligation is to risk the possible ineffectiveness of executions. However rationalized, the opposite view appears to be motivated by the simple fact that executions are more subjected to social control than murder. However, this applies to all penalties and does not argue for the abolition of any.

5

The Risk of Executing the Innocent Makes the Death Penalty Unfair

Joseph P. Shapiro

Joseph P. Shapiro, an award-winning journalist, currently serves as the science correspondent for National Public Radio (NPR). Prior to joining NPR in 2001, Shapiro wrote about social policy issues for U.S. News & World Report.

Many Americans who support the death penalty assume that those sentenced to die are guilty. However, a growing number of wrongful convictions challenge the fairness of capital punishment. False confessions and discarded evidence are responsible for some of these wrongful convictions. However, the main reason people are wrongfully convicted is poor legal representation. Because the current legal system is flawed, the death penalty is unjust.

G ary Gauger's voice was flat when he called 911 to report finding his father in a pool of blood. Police arrived at the Illinois farmhouse Gauger shared with his parents and discovered that his mother was dead, too. The 40-year-old son, a quirky ex-hippie organic farmer, became a murder suspect. After all, someone had slashed Ruth and Morrie Gauger's throats just 30 feet from where Gary slept. There were no signs of a struggle or robbery. But what most bothered the cops was the son's reaction: He quietly tended to his tomato plants as they investigated. Eventually, Gauger was sentenced to die by lethal

Joseph P. Shapiro, "The Wrong Men on Death Row," *U.S. News & World Report*, vol. 125, November 9, 1998. Copyright © 1998 by *U.S. News & World Report*. Reproduced by permission.

injection—until it became clear police had the wrong guy. His case is not unusual.

After years of debate, most Americans now believe the death penalty is an appropriate punishment for the most repulsive murders. But that support is rooted in an underlying assumption: that the right person is being executed. The most recent list by an antideath-penalty group shows that Gary Gauger is one of 74 men exonerated and freed from death row over the past 25 years—a figure so stark it's causing even some supporters of capital punishment to rethink whether the death penalty can work fairly. Among them is Gerald Kogan, who recently stepped down as chief justice of Florida's Supreme Court. "If one innocent person is executed along the way, then we can no longer justify capital punishment," he says.

Mistaken convictions

For every 7 executions—486 since 1976—1 other prisoner on death row has been found innocent. And there's concern even more mistaken convictions will follow as record numbers of inmates fill death rows, pressure builds for speedy executions, and fewer attorneys defend prisoners facing execution. . . .

> *Gauger was sentenced to die by lethal injection—until it became clear police had the wrong guy.*

Timeout sought. Executions have been rare since the death penalty was reinstated in 1976. But the pace is picking up. There are now [in 1997] 3,517 prisoners on death row in the 38 capital-punishment states—an all-time high and a tripling since 1982. The 74 executions in 1997—the most since 1955—represented a 60 percent spike from the year before. Citing bad lawyering and mistaken convictions, the American Bar Association in 1997 called for a death-penalty moratorium. This month, Illinois legislators will vote on such a ban.[1] That state, more than any other, is grappling with the problem: It has exonerated al-

1. In 2000 Illinois governor George Ryan imposed a moratorium on executions in Illinois.

most as many men (9) on death row as it has executed (11).

It's tempting to view the reprieved as proof that the legal system eventually corrects its mistakes. But only one of the nine men released in Illinois got out through normal appeals. Most have outsiders to thank. Northwestern University journalism professor David Protess and four of his students followed leads missed by police and defense attorneys to tie four other men to the rape and murders that put four innocent men in prison. "Without them, I'd be in the graveyard," says Dennis Williams, who spent 16 years on death row. "The system didn't do anything."

> *Only one of the nine men released in Illinois got out through normal appeals.*

Most damning of the current system would be proof that a guiltless person has been executed. Credible, but not clear-cut, claims of innocence have been raised in a handful of executions since 1976. Leonel Herrera died by lethal injection in Texas in 1993 even though another man confessed to the murder. The U.S. Supreme Court ruled that, with his court appeals exhausted, an extraordinary amount of proof was required to stop his execution. Governors, the court noted, can still grant clemency in such cases. But what was once common is now so politically risky that only about one death row inmate a year wins such freedom.

How wrongful convictions happen

Gary Gauger's calm gave a cop a hunch. But it was Gauger's trusting nature that gave police a murder tale that day in 1993. Gauger says that during 18 hours of nonstop interrogation, detectives insisted they had a "stack of evidence" against him. They didn't—but it never occurred to the laid-back farmer that his accusers might be lying. Instead, he worried he might have blacked out the way he sometimes did in the days when he drank heavily. So Gauger went along with police suggestions that, to jog his memory, he hypothetically describe the murders. After viewing photos of his mother's slit throat, Gauger explained how he could have walked into her rug shop next to the house ("she knows and trusts me"), pulled her hair, slashed her throat and then done the same to his dad as he worked in his nearby antique-motorcycle shop. To police, this was a chilling confession. Even Gauger, by this point suicidal, believed he must have committed the crimes.

False confessions

Though police failed to turn up any physical evidence during a 10-day search of the farm, prosecutors depicted Gauger as an oddball who could have turned on his mother and father. He was a pot-smoking ex-alcoholic who once lived on a commune and brought his organic farming ways back to Richmond, Ill. The judge rolled his eyes during Gauger's testimony and, when defense attorneys objected, simply turned his back on Gauger. The jury took just three hours to reach a guilty verdict. "Nutty as a fruitcake," the jury foreman declared afterward.

A study by Profs. Hugo Bedau of Tufts University and Michael Radelet of the University of Florida found three factors common among wrongful capital convictions. One third involve perjured testimony, often from jailhouse snitches claiming to have heard a defendant's prison confession. (At Gauger's trial, a fellow inmate made a dubious claim to hearing Gauger confess. The man, contacted in jail by *U.S. News & World Report*, offered to tell a very different story if the magazine would pay for an interview.) One of every 7 cases, Bedau and Radelet found, involves faulty eyewitness identifications, and a seventh involve false confessions, like Gauger's.

> *The falsely convicted is almost always an outsider—often from a minority group.*

False confessions occur with greater frequency than recognized even by law-enforcement professionals, argues Richard Leo of the University of California, Irvine. About a quarter, he estimates, involve people with mild mental retardation, who often try to hide limitations by guessing "right" answers to police questions. Children are vulnerable, too. Chicago police in September dropped murder charges against two boys, 7 and 8 years old, who confessed to killing 11-year-old Ryan Harris with a rock to steal her bicycle. After a crime laboratory found semen on the dead girl's clothes, police began looking for an older suspect. An educated innocent person, likely to trust police, may be especially prone to police trickery—which courts allow as often necessary to crack savvy criminals. "My parents had just been murdered and these were the good guys," Gauger says. "I know it sounds naive now, but when they told me they wouldn't lie to me, I believed them."

The falsely convicted is almost always an outsider—often from a minority group. In Illinois, six of the nine dismissed from death row were black or Hispanic men accused of murder, rape, or both of white victims. But the No. 1 reason people are falsely convicted is poor legal representation. Many states cap fees for court-appointed attorneys, which makes it tough for indigents to get competent lawyers. And it's been harder for inmates to find lawyers to handle appeals since Congress in 1996 stopped funding legal-aid centers in 20 states.

How wrongful convictions get discovered

Gary Gauger has a simple answer to how he won his freedom: "I got lucky." Of all the 74 released from death row, Gauger's stay was one of the briefest—just eight months. Shortly after his conviction, FBI agents listening in on a wiretap overheard members of a motorcycle gang discussing the murder of Ruth and Morrie Gauger. In 1997, two members of the Outlaws Motorcycle Club, Randall "Madman" Miller and James "Preacher" Schneider, were indicted for the Gauger killings. But a federal judge in 1998 ruled the wiretaps were unauthorized and dismissed all the charges. . . .

Even when another person confesses, the legal system can be slow to respond. Rolando Cruz and Alejandro Hernandez spent 10 years each on death row in Illinois for the rape and murder of 10-year-old Jeanine Nicarico. Shortly after their convictions, police arrested a repeat sex offender and murderer named Brian Dugan who confessed to the crime, providing minute details unknown to the public. Prosecutors still insisted Cruz and Hernandez were the killers—even after DNA testing linked Dugan to the crime. At Cruz's third trial, a police officer admitted that he'd lied when he testified Cruz had confessed in a "vision" about the girl's murder. The judge then declared Cruz not guilty. In January [1999], seven police officers and prosecutors go on trial charged with conspiracy to conceal and fabricate evidence against Cruz and Hernandez.[2]

DNA profiling, perhaps more than any other development, has exposed the fallibility of the legal system. In the last decade [1988 to 1998], 56 wrongfully convicted people have won release because of DNA testing, 10 of them from death row.[3] Attorneys Barry Scheck and Peter Neufeld, with the help of their students at New York's Cardozo School of Law, have freed 35 of those. But their Innocence Project has been hobbled by the fact that, in 70 percent of the cases they pursued police had already discarded semen, hair, or other evidence needed for testing.

Gauger had one other thing going for him that is key to overturning bogus convictions: outside advocates. Most important was his twin sister, Ginger, who convinced Northwestern Law School Prof. Lawrence Marshall (who also defended Cruz) to help her brother a week before the deadline for the final state appeal. In September 1994, Gauger's death sentence was reduced to life in prison. Two years later, he was freed. Marshall visited Gauger in prison with the surprise news. "That's good," he said with a smile and his customary calm.

It's a fall afternoon and starlings are fluttering through the colorful maples that frame the Gauger farmhouse. Gary Gauger loads a dusty pickup with pumpkins, squash, and other vegetables. Inside, Ginger has taken up her mother's business of selling Asian kilims [woven rugs] and American Indian pottery. A friend runs the vintage-motorcycle business, still called Morrie's Place, in an adjoining garage. For Gary Gauger, life seems normal again. Customers at his vegetable stand sort through bushels of squash. A hand-lettered sign advises: "Self Service: please place money in black box . . . thanks."

But there is pain, too, for his lost parents and for his 3½ lost years. Gauger says the worst part about being wrongfully convicted is knowing that the guilty person is free. The victim Gauger most thinks about is 7-year-old Melissa Ackerman. The little girl was grabbed from her bicycle, sodomized, and left in an irrigation ditch, her body so unrecognizable that she could be identified only by dental records. She was killed by Brian Dugan, while Rolando Cruz and Alejandro Hernandez sat behind bars—falsely convicted of another child's murder committed by Dugan.

---

1. Cruz and Hernandez were cleared of criminal charges and pardoned in 2002.
2. As this volume went to press, 145 wrongly convicted people had been released because of DNA testing. Seventy-three of them had been on death row.

6

Capital Punishment Is a Just Consequence for Those Who Choose Evil

Gregory Koukl

Gregory Koukl is a prolific author, radio show host, and public speaker. He is president and founder of Stand to Reason, a Christian group dedicated to promoting understanding of Christian principles.

Opponents of the death penalty often argue that people commit crimes because they have suffered from bad past circumstances, such as childhood abuse. However, this reasoning is wrong because human beings are free moral agents who can make choices, and they need to be held accountable for the choices they make. By punishing criminals, society reaffirms that individuals do not have to react mechanistically to their past but are capable of choosing between good and evil.

I've been looking for an opportunity to comment on a *Los Angeles Times* letter to the editor from mid-January [1996]. I think it's the right time now because of the recent execution of William Bonin, the freeway killer. Though there are hundreds of people on death row, this is only the third execution in California since the renewal of capital punishment. William Bonin was executed by lethal injection, not by the gas chamber. There's a belief that this is more humane. I thought it was interesting, in reading the accounts of the execution, that nothing was said about the process or manner of death other than that it was by lethal injection. Generally, there is a long, boring

Gregory Koukl, "Capital Punishment: Is Man a Machine or a Moral Agent?" www. str.org, Stand to Reason, March 22, 1996. Copyright © 1996 by Gregory Koukl. Reproduced by permission.

description of the painful process of death a person goes through in the gas chamber. California now considers the gas chamber cruel and unusual punishment so they have gone to lethal injection. I think that's fine. I'm for capital punishment. One of the reasons is because I think it gives us an opportunity for moral clarity with regards to the punishment issue. This brings up the piece I saw in the *Los Angeles Times* in mid-January. The writer, Robert Finn, makes this comment: "*Times* editors place the continuation of an article on California's upcoming first execution by lethal injection right next to an article on Israeli President Azar Wiseman's visit to a former Nazi death camp near Berlin. Now whether intentional or not, this juxtaposition serves as a reminder that even legal execution is murder, a fact that no amount of technological improvement can mask. Whether the government kills millions of innocent Jews or a single vicious and unrepentant murderer, the death penalty diminishes us all." Signed Robert Finn, Long Beach.

This was one of those pieces that stands out for me as an example of a lack of moral clarity—an inability to make valuable moral distinctions regarding behavior. Of course, I expect such a thing in a culture that is run through and through with relativistic thinking, and has a view of man that diminishes him to a mere machine. The language of this letter to the editor, the juxtaposition of this article about capital punishment by lethal injection and the other article about Wiseman's visit to a Nazi death camp, equates the two as if they were morally equivalent. He equates the execution of a vicious and unrepentant murderer with the killing of innocent Jews. Apparently, Robert Finn can't distinguish between guilt and innocence, even when it is in his own writing.

> *I think that human beings are free moral agents. They can make choices and they ought to be held responsible for the moral choices they make.*

There is a moral distinction. It isn't the same to kill an innocent person as it is for the state to properly execute someone who is guilty. I have heard quite a number of arguments against capital punishment. I've spent a lot of time discussing and even debating this issue. I have noticed a couple of things about those who argue against capital punishment, *per se*. I think there may be some arguments against capital punishment which question the way it is executed, whether it is just and whether everybody has an equal chance. I understand that people like [Christian writer and radio host] Chuck Colson are against capital punishment because of certain inequities in the system. But that is a different kind of objection. This objection is different from the person who objects to capital punishment, *per se*. That is someone who objects to capital punishment in itself, who believes there is no circumstance in any kind of situation in which capital punishment is a justified form of punishment. Those who argue against capital punishment, *per se*, argue based on a couple of different things. All of those arguments make a principal error. The error they make is in their assessment of what it means to be a human being.

"What kind of being is man?"

As I read the account of the Bonin execution yesterday morning, there were comments about Bonin's life—his abuse-ridden childhood, the difficulties he faced growing up, his experience as a Viet Nam war vet which suggested that might have influenced his behavior. Similar kinds of arguments came up when Robert Alton Harris [convicted of murdering two boys] faced execution. One of the strongest appeals made by the defense had to do with an alleged fetal alcohol syndrome of Harris. Apparently his mother was an alcoholic and there was some evidence that her alcoholic condition influenced his development as an unborn child. The underlying argument was that if there are factors that compel a person's actions then they ought to be considered mitigating circumstances in his punishment.

I have two thoughts about this and each of them, I think, is very, very important. The first one has to do with our view of man. Before we resolve the question of how we ought to deal with human beings who do bad things, we have to ask the question, "What kind of being is man?" I realize that some of you may think that is too philosophical. But, in fact, you have already answered the question based on the kind of response you give to the capital punishment question. If you are taken by these kinds of argument—fetal alcohol syndrome, bad environment, Viet Nam war, child abuse, things that may dispose a person to certain immoral or antisocial conduct—then that tells me that your view of man is very mechanistic. In other words, you view human beings, by and large, as machines and not as moral agents. What happens when a machine goes bad? Do we punish the machine? Of course not. We fix the machine. If the machine can't be fixed, we discard it. Or, if in the case of an animal, we will remove the animal or kill the animal. Not because it is guilty and it ought to be punished because we don't hold them morally responsible since moral terms don't seem to really apply to animals. But we remove it from any position of being able to do harm to others in society. The underlying point of view or philosophy about the nature of man is what seems to form our decisions about capital punishment. That's why people use defenses against capital punishment like this one: "It doesn't do any good because, first of all, you can't reform a dead man and, secondly, it is not a deterrent for other people committing the crime in the future." You see, what this argument amounts to is a pre-commitment to the idea that any action the state should take with regards to a person committing a crime should be actions that fix the problem, repair the machine, or at least influence other machines not to go bad in the future. That's why we have the idea of reform at the heart of much of our penal system, at least philosophically. It doesn't work out that way a lot, but rehabilitation is the idea. Michael Jackson—talk show host in Southern California on a secular station—argued last week [1996] that if we are executing someone just to get back at the person who committed the crime, then that is not justice, it's vengeance. Furthermore, capital punishment doesn't work to deter crime. Therefore, since we shouldn't be vengeful and since we should work to deter crime in the future, capital punishment is not justifiable.

> **❝** *If man is not responsible such that he is not deserving of capital punishment, then how is he deserving of any punishment whatsoever?* **❞**

I don't think those arguments work. The reason I don't think they work is because I have a different view of man. I do not believe that man is a machine. I think that human beings are free moral agents. They can make choices and they ought to be held responsible for the moral choices they make. This means two things. First, if people make good choices and make a worthwhile, virtuous contribution to the world, then that means we ought to praise them. And praise we do, oftentimes. I was on a show recently, a secular station, in which others were talking with vibrant praise for [professional basketball player] Magic Johnson for his contribution to society, his return to the sport and all the good that would do. He was a hero in their minds. Notice there was no problem with attributing praise to Magic Johnson because it seems that when someone does something good, he ought to be praised. That only works when someone can choose their actions. Therefore they are praised for making the right choice. But these same people who make bad choices ought not to be praised, but rather punished. Keep in mind the praise is not just so other people will do good things in the future. We are praising him as a good example to cause other people to act in a certain way. We hope that will happen. We hold up other individuals who are noble and virtuous as role models. But the praise is an end in itself because we think it is valuable to praise the individual for the good that he has done.

Secondly, if that is true, then on the other side of the coin that person who was worthy of praise for its own sake when doing something good is also worthy of blame, and therefore punishment, when he does bad. Not merely reform, but punishment for what he did wrong. And the punishment should fit the crime. We are not just to be concerned with rehabilitation, fixing the machine and influencing other people not to do bad in the future. So when somebody commits a capital crime, we are actually making a statement about the high level of value of human individuals who were made in the image of God, but nonetheless have the capability of choosing good and evil. We are acknowledging the meaningfulness of that individual's choice when we praise them for good things but also when we punish them for bad things.

Responsibility and anti–death penalty arguments

My comments are meant to make the point that policy issues and ethical positions need to be informed by deeper philosophic commitments. In this case, the view of punishment vs. rehabilitation, retribution vs. rehabilitation, will ultimately hinge on how you view man. Is man a machine or is man a moral agent worthy of praise and punishment? I think many people are straddling those two views. They want to treat man like he's worthy of praise then treat him like a machine when it comes to the issue of punishment, saying we shouldn't punish people because it's revenge. Well, yeah, that's right. It is social revenge. No apologies. Justice is a kind of revenge. It is getting back, but it is an appropriate getting back when executed by the appropriate authorities. In this case, the state. The state has an interest in getting revenge. God has given them that responsibility. He has extended the responsibility to them to wield the sword on His behalf for the purpose of punishing evil doers. It says that very clearly in the Scriptures. In Romans 13 it also says to praise those who do right. What they want to do, though, is object to the punishment thing and say man is not responsible for his actions because there are extenuating circumstances. It was these extenuating circumstances that were the deciding factors that caused someone to do bad when they could not have done otherwise. Since something else caused them, something else is responsible, so we ought not punish them in this way. Of course, the argument breaks down because when the time comes around for praise, then the rules change. Then all of a sudden people are responsible for their behavior. It seems to me people either are responsible or they are not. If they are responsible, then both praise and punishment make sense. If they are not responsible, then let's get rid of punishment but let's get rid of praise, too. This is why [behavioral psychologist] B.F. Skinner was at least intellectually honest when he wrote his book, *Beyond Freedom and Dignity*, arguing that the environment controls all of our behaviors and is ultimately deterministic. If that is the case then we ought not be praised nor should we be punished. We should just be manipulated as machines so that we work better for the good of all. Of course, then you've got a problem of defining what this word "good" means in a mechanistic environment. My view is that man is not a machine. That is why it doesn't matter whether someone is reformed or not. If they are properly punished then the goal of punishment is fulfilled. Retribution. I think that it's noble in cases where there can be some reform and moral training to make someone a better person. But I don't want the tail to wag the dog. That's secondary to the question of punishment.

The other problem with this view, and I hinted at it just a few moments ago, is that it seems to prove too much. If man is not responsible such that he is not deserving of capital punishment, then how is he deserving of any punishment whatsoever? Last time we had an execution, [world-famous advocate for the poor] Mother Teresa, I think, was misdirected on this issue. She called the governor's office and pleaded with [California] Governor [Pete] Wilson for the life of Robert Alton Harris. Mother Teresa's argument was that Jesus would forgive him. Well, I agree with her on that. If he fulfilled the requirements for forgiveness, Jesus would forgive him. But I'm not sure what that has to do with the question of how the government ought to treat a criminal. If it is true that Jesus would forgive him and that is a good argument against capital punishment in his case, then what are we to do with Robert Alton Harris, or William Bonin, or anyone else in a similar situation? Mother Teresa's suggestion was to just let him stay in prison for the rest of his life. This is what many people suggest as an alternative. My response to that is going to be Mother Teresa's response. But Jesus would forgive him. Or the secular version, he had fetal alcohol syndrome so he wasn't really culpable. Maybe he should just do 10 years. But he wasn't culpable and Jesus would forgive. Maybe one year. Maybe one month. Even for one day. If the man is not culpable because there are extenuating circumstances, he ought not be in prison even for a day. If we release him from capital punishment because Jesus would forgive, then we can't justify, based on the same reasoning, any punishment whatsoever.

This is the problem with most of these arguments. They prove too much. They apply with equal force not just to capital punishment but to any punishment whatsoever. If those are good arguments, they require that we simply dismantle the legal system. If we are going to treat men as machines, or at best as sick animals who need to get better, then putting them in prison certainly is not the way to heal them. We would rather then commit ourselves to the kind of environment that would make them the most docile and most law-abiding. Maybe we should just put them in a resort and provide for all of their needs and make their lives wonderful and pay their way through college so that they are changed into law-abiding citizens. Then they are no longer even tempted to do bad if they are mere machines to be fixed, or non-moral, non-responsible animals to be rehabilitated. Why prison at all? Nobody wants to do that for the same reason they feel comfortable receiving praise. They understand deep within them that man is a moral animal who is responsible and who ought to be praised when he does good, but who ought to be punished when he does wrong.

7

Women Are Often Unfairly Spared the Death Penalty

Thad Rueter

Thad Rueter is a staff writer for the Daytona Beach News-Journal.

Women are rarely put on death row, and few are actually executed. These trends stem in part from society's perception that women are less threatening and violent than men. Prosecutors of women defendants in capital cases have to try to "defeminize" them by portraying them as lesbians, gang leaders, or violent characters who defy traditional female stereotypes. It is unlikely that the gender bias in death penalty sentencing will disappear any time soon.

The facts are simple. In 1977, Guinevere Garcia murdered her daughter, and later received a 10-year sentence for the killing. Four months after her release, she killed her estranged husband during a robbery attempt. This time, the court imposed the death penalty.

Garcia had refused to appeal her sentence, and opposed efforts [of others] to save her. Death penalty opponents turned to Illinois Gov. Jim Edgar, who, as a state legislator, voted to restore the death penalty.

The facts of the case swayed his opinion. Just hours before the scheduled execution, Edgar commuted Garcia's sentence to life without parole, his first such act in more than five years in office.

The fact that Garcia escaped her execution isn't so unusual.

Since the beginning of the colonial era, 20,000 people have been lawfully executed in America, but only 400 of them have been women, including 27 who were found guilty of witchcraft. In the . . . years since the Supreme Court reinstated capital punishment, [at least] 5,569 total death sentences have been given out by courts, 112 to women. Of these 112, only one has been executed (Velma Barfield in 1984), compared with 301 men.[1]

Expectations of the female gender

Leigh Beinen, a Northwestern University law professor who studies the gender bias in capital cases nationwide, thinks the reason so few women face execution has to do with the symbolism that's central to the death penalty.

"Capital punishment is about portraying people as devils," she says. "But women are usually seen as less threatening."

Juries and judges tend to find more mitigating factors in capital cases involving women than in ones involving men, Beinen explains. Women who kill abusive spouses, for example, are often seen as victims. Women are more likely to kill someone they know without any premeditation, which is considered less serious than killing a stranger, while some women are presented by defense attorneys as operating under the domination of men. And Garcia's case, according to Edgar, was not "the worst of the worst."

> *Juries and judges tend to find more mitigating factors in capital cases involving women than in ones involving men.*

"Putting women in docks provokes community ambivalence," says Beinen, pointing out that by the end of the Susan Smith trial last year [1995], which left the young mother convicted of drowning her two toddler sons, initial demands for the death penalty had largely petered out.

Victor Streib, a leading expert on gender bias, has shown

1. Since this article was originally published, at least nine more women have been executed.

that while women comprise 13 percent of U.S. murder arrests, they account for only 2 percent of the death sentences, and make up only 1.5 percent of all persons presently on death row. These last two figures have remained steady for 20 years.

> *While women comprise 13 percent of U.S. murder arrests, they account for only 2 percent of the death sentences, and make up only 1.5 percent of all persons presently on death row.*

Streib says prosecutors try to "defeminize" defendants by portraying them as lesbians—even if they're not—or prone to violence, gang leaders or having other traits contrary to "natural female patterns." But prosecutors still have a tough time overcoming defense tactics that include profuse crying, bodily shaking and a head hung in shame, histrionics that disturb Streib.

"It lumps women in with the retarded and children by implying that they can't control their own actions," he says.

Fixing the problem

Streib, who teaches at Cleveland-Marshall College of Law, and has compiled three studies of gender bias in capital punishment, has spoken before groups opposed to the death penalty, but says they haven't used his research because they are afraid of "stirring the pot" by giving aid to death penalty advocates. Anyway, he says, he's a scholar, not a politician, and his goal is to "explain the unexplained" and provide ammunition for the debate.

Beinen makes no secret of her opposition to capital punishment, and says she was "happy" to see Garcia's sentence commuted. Beinen has received a few letters from men who are fighting their death sentences on the grounds of gender bias, but though she says the death penalty is unfair, she is pessimistic about these challenges.

Gender bias challenges would run into the same obstacles as racial challenges, Streib says. In *McCleskey v. Kemp* [1987], the Supreme Court ruled that death-row defendants cannot argue a general pattern of racial bias in capital cases. Instead, a defendant must prove that race affected his or her specific case, a precedent that Streib thinks will block any gender suit. He predicts someone will push legislative action dealing with gender bias, and that it will be something along the lines of the failed Racial Justice Act, which would have allowed capital defendants to use statistics to challenge race bias.

"But it's not likely there will be a cure," he says.

So will anything change? Probably not, according to Streib. Because of the powerful symbolism of execution, he doesn't think the rising anti-crime mood of the country will lead to any great increase in the number of women on death row. And while Beinen hopes that gender-bias research will make people aware that capital punishment is all about "symbolism and politics," Streib is more guarded.

"We'll probably have another execution in the next 23 years," he says. "I expect one soon, but I've been saying that for a while now."

8

Racist Courts Make Capital Punishment Extremely Unjust for African American Defendants

Richard C. Dieter

Richard C. Dieter is an attorney and the executive director of the Death Penalty Information Center, a nonprofit organization founded in 1990 to gather and disseminate information about the death penalty.

African Americans who are accused of committing capital crimes are often treated unfairly because the justice system is racist. National studies show that they are sentenced to death much more frequently than defendants of other races who have committed similar crimes. Lawyers and jurors are predominantly white men who are more likely to seek the death penalty for African American defendants than for white ones. The American death penalty system therefore violates human rights.

The results of two new studies which underscore the continuing injustice of racism in the application of the death penalty are being released through this report. The first study documents the infectious presence of racism in the death penalty, and demonstrates that this problem has not slackened with time, nor is it restricted to a single region of the country. The other study identifies one of the potential causes for this continuing crisis: those who are making the critical death penalty decisions in this country are almost exclusively white. . . .

These new empirical studies underscore a persistent pattern of racial disparities which has appeared throughout the country over the past twenty years. Examinations of the relationship between race and the death penalty, with varying levels of thoroughness and sophistication, have now been conducted in every major death penalty state. In 96% of these reviews, there was a pattern of either race-of-victim or race-of-defendant discrimination, or both. The gravity of the close connection between race and the death penalty is shown when compared to studies in other fields. Race is more likely to affect death sentencing than smoking affects the likelihood of dying from heart disease. The latter evidence has produced enormous changes in law and societal practice, while racism in the death penalty has been largely ignored. . . .

The human cost of this racial injustice is incalculable. The decisions about who lives and who dies are being made along racial lines by a nearly all white group of prosecutors. The death penalty presents a stark symbol of the effects of racial discrimination. In individual cases, this racism is reflected in ethnic slurs hurled at black defendants by the prosecution and even by the defense. It results in black jurors being systematically barred from service, and in the devoting of more resources to white victims of homicide at the expense of black victims. And it results in a death penalty in which blacks are frequently put to death for murdering whites, but whites are almost never executed for murdering blacks. Such a system of injustice is not merely unfair and unconstitutional—it tears at the very principles to which this country struggles to adhere. . . .

Study I: The Philadelphia story

More than half of the death sentences rendered in Pennsylvania are cases from Philadelphia, a city with only 14% of the state's population. Philadelphia's District Attorney, Lynne Abraham, has been called "The Deadliest D.A." in a 1995 *New York Times* article. Eighty-three percent of those on death row from Philadelphia are African-American. But raw numbers of racial disproportion do not tell the whole story. In order to determine for certain whether race is a decisive factor, researchers must examine the outcomes in cases of similar severity with defendants of similar criminal backgrounds.

This examination requires a statistical analysis which takes into account such factors as multiple victims, the deliberate infliction of pain, and the background of the accused. The ultimate question is: "Among similar cases, is race a factor in whether death sentences are imposed against black defendants?"

Such a study was recently conducted in Philadelphia. The results are dramatic, particularly for a state outside of the deep south, a region where racial disparities in the criminal justice system have a long history. The researchers examined a large sample of the murders which were eligible for the death penalty in the state between 1983 and 1993. The researchers found that, even after controlling for case differences, *blacks in Philadelphia were substantially more likely to get the death penalty* than other defendants who committed similar murders. Black defendants faced odds of receiving a death sentence that were 3.9 times higher than other similarly situated defendants.

> *The death penalty presents a stark symbol of the effects of racial discrimination.*

The researchers used a variety of analytical tools to compare and validate their findings. They consistently found substantial race-of-defendant disparities. The results of this bias against black defendants in Philadelphia is estimated to be an *excess of 38% in death sentences for black defendants compared to all other defendants for similar crimes. . . .*

Whichever measures the researchers employed, the statistics pointed to the same conclusion: black defendants on average face a distinctly higher risk of receiving a death sentence than all other similarly situated defendants. The various independent tests were so thoroughly consistent that they pointed to race discrimination as the underlying cause. The researchers stated: "In the face of these results, we consider it implausible that the estimated disparities are a product of chance or reflect a failure to control for important omitted case characteristics. . . . In short, we believe it would be extremely unlikely to observe disparities of this magnitude and consistency if there were substantial equality in the treatment of defendants in this system."

For those on death row from Philadelphia, these numbers

translate into a harsh and deadly reality: if the death penalty were applied to blacks as it is to others, there would be far fewer blacks facing execution. . . .

If the racial disparities documented in the study of capital cases in Philadelphia were unique, they might be dismissed as simply a local problem requiring a local solution. But such racial patterns have appeared in study after study all over the country and over an extensive period of time.

> *Despite these pervasive patterns implying racial discrimination, courts have been closed to challenges raising this issue.*

In the late 1980s, Congress asked the General Accounting Office (GAO) to review the empirical studies on race and the death penalty which had been conducted up to that time. The agency reviewed 28 studies regarding both race-of-defendant and race-of-victim discrimination. Their review included studies utilizing various methodologies and degrees of statistical sophistication and examined such diverse states as California, Florida, Georgia, Illinois, Kentucky, Louisiana, Mississippi, New Jersey, and Texas. Their conclusion in 1990, based on the vast amount of data collected, was unequivocal:

> In 82% of the studies, race of victim was found to influence the likelihood of being charged with capital murder or receiving a death sentence, i.e., *those who murdered whites were found to be more likely to be sentenced to death than those who murdered blacks.* This finding was remarkably consistent across data sets, states, data collection methods, and analytic techniques. The finding held for high, medium, and low quality studies. . . .

A particularly egregious example of race of victim discrimination was revealed in a recent review of the cases from Kentucky's death row. Researchers at the University of Louisville had found in 1995 that, as in other states, blacks who killed whites were more likely to receive the death penalty than any other offender-victim combination. In fact, looking at the makeup of Kentucky's death row in 1996 revealed that 100% of the inmates were there for murdering a white victim, and none were there for the murder of a black victim, despite the fact that there have been over 1,000 African-Americans murdered in Kentucky since the death penalty was reinstated. This gross disparity among capital cases sends a message that the taking of a white life is more serious than the taking of a black life, and that Kentucky's courts hand out death sentences on that basis.

This biased use of the death penalty for the murder of those in the white community, but not those in the black community, led to the introduction of legislation allowing consideration of such patterns of racial disparities. The bill, referred to as the "Racial Justice Act," failed in the Kentucky legislature in 1996, but was passed in 1998. It will permit race-based challenges to prosecutorial decisions to seek a death sentence.

No relief in the courts

Despite these pervasive patterns implying racial discrimination, courts have been closed to challenges raising this issue. In *McCleskey v. Kemp*, the U.S. Supreme Court held that the defendant had to show that he was personally discriminated against in the course of the prosecution. "Merely" showing a disturbing pattern of racial disparities in Georgia over a long period of time was not sufficient to prove bias in his case.

The federal courts have taken their cue from *McCleskey* and have not granted relief based on a racial application of the death penalty in *any* case. When such claims of racial bias are raised in civil rights suits alleging employment or housing discrimination, civil rights legislation instructs the courts to employ a more commonsensical burden of proof and provides a chance for relief. In criminal cases, however, the courts require the defense to "get inside" the mind of the prosecutor or jury and show purposeful race discrimination directed at the defendant, an almost impossible task. . . .

Study II: The race of the decision makers

As the analysis above indicates, racially biased decisions can readily enter the criminal justice system through the discretion given to prosecutors to selectively seek the death penalty in some cases but not others. The GAO review of race discrimination noted that "race of victim influence was found at all stages of the criminal justice process" and that "the evidence for the race of victim influence was stronger for the earlier stages of the judicial process (e.g., prosecutorial decision to charge the defendant with a capital offense, decision to proceed to trial rather than plea bargain) than in later stages."

The death penalty could be sought in far more cases than it actually is, and prosecutors use a variety of factors to determine which cases are deserving of the state's worst punishment. That discretion more likely results in capital prosecutions when the victim in the underlying murder is white, and in some states, when the defendant is black. Except for extreme cases, as when a black police officer is killed, the murder of people of color is not treated as seriously as the murder of white people.

> *Judges, defense attorneys and jurors can also display harmful racial bias.*

One of the likely reasons for this discrepancy is that *almost all the prosecutors making the key decision about whether death will be sought are white*. . . .

Professor Jeffrey Pokorak of St. Mary's University School of Law collected data regarding the race and gender of the government officials empowered to prosecute criminal offenses, and in particular, capital offenses from all 38 states that use the death penalty. The study was concluded in February, 1998.

It revealed that only 1% of the District Attorneys in death penalty states in this country are black and only 1% are Hispanic. The remaining 97.5% are white, and almost all of them are male. . . .

The implications of this study go far beyond the shocking numbers and racial isolation of those in this key law enforcement position. When a prosecutor is faced with a crime in his community, he often consults with the family of the victim as to whether the death penalty should be sought. If the victim's family is prominent, white, and likely to support him in his next election, there may be a greater willingness to expend the extensive financial resources and time which a death penalty prosecution will take.

The way that racial bias can play out in practice is illustrated by one of the key death penalty jurisdictions in the country: Georgia's Chattahoochee Judicial District, which has sent more people to death row than any other district in the state. In a recent law review article, Stephen Bright, of the Southern Center for Human Rights in Atlanta, described the prosecutor's practice there:

> An investigation of all murder cases prosecuted . . . from 1973 to 1990 revealed that in cases involving the murder of a white person, prosecutors often met with the victim's family and discussed whether to seek the death penalty. In a case involving the murder of the daughter of a prominent white contractor, the prosecutor contacted the contractor and asked him if he wanted to seek the death penalty. When the contractor replied in the affirmative, the prosecutor said that was all he needed to know. He obtained the death penalty at trial. He was rewarded with a contribution of $5,000 from the contractor when he successfully ran for judge in the next election. The contribution was the largest received by the District Attorney. There were other cases in which the District Attorney issued press releases announcing that he was seeking the death penalty after meeting with the family of a white victim. But *prosecutors failed to meet with African-Americans whose family members had been murdered to determine what sentence they wanted.* Most were not even notified that the case had been resolved. As a result of these practices, although African-Americans were the victims of 65% of the homicides in the Chattahoochee Judicial District, 85% of the capital cases were white victim cases.

Racial bias permeates the system

Prosecutors not only decide who should be charged with a particular level of offense, they also have a significant impact on the way the trial is conducted. When a prosecutor refers to an Hispanic defendant as "a chili-eating bastard," as happened in a Colorado death penalty case, it sets a tone of acceptance of racial prejudice for the entire trial. Similarly, the selection of juries is an essential part of this process, and some prosecutors have made a practice of eliminating blacks from their prospective juries, thereby increasing the likelihood of a race-based decision. . . .

These same practices are common in other jurisdictions. According to a recent federal court decision in Alabama reviewing a death penalty case, the Tuscaloosa District Attorney's Office had a "standard operating procedure . . . to use the peremptory challenges to strike as many blacks as possible from the venires in cases involving serious crimes.". . .

Evidence of racial discrimination in the U.S. death penalty system has attracted worldwide attention.

Prosecutors are not alone in acting out of racial prejudice. Judges, defense attorneys and jurors can also display harmful racial bias. It is the defendant, however, who suffers the consequences. In the death penalty trial of Ramon Mata in Texas, the prosecutor and the defense attorney agreed to excuse all prospective minority race jurors, thereby ensuring an all white jury. The U.S. Court of Appeals for the Fifth Circuit found this to be harmless error. . . .

Public reaction

After the Civil War and the emancipation of the slaves, lynchings of black people were common in the U.S. From the late 1800s, at least 4,743 people were killed by lynch mobs, with 90% of the lynchings occurring in the South, and most of the victims being black people. Lynchings were praised as necessary and just, and even some governors deferred to the public demand for vengeance. Georgia populist Tom Watson observed that "Lynch law is a good sign; it shows that a sense of justice yet lives among the people."

Revulsion at the spectacle and gross injustices of the lynching era eventually led to the formation of the National Association for the Advancement of Colored People and then to the demise of lynching. But the disparities evident in today's death penalty indicate that prejudice and racism remain a potent force infecting our system of justice.

These racial disparities in capital punishment have drawn increasingly critical reaction from legal and civil rights groups both nationally and internationally. After the Supreme Court narrowly rejected a challenge to the racially biased application of the death penalty in Georgia, civil rights groups and many newspaper editorials called for the passage of the Racial Justice Act to remedy this injustice on a national level. Although this proposed legislation was passed by the U.S. House of Representatives in 1994 and 1990, it was ultimately defeated on the theory that such a racial inquiry would "abolish" the death penalty. Only Kentucky has passed similar legislation on the state level.

As a result of this and other inequities in the administration of capital punishment, the ABA [American Bar Association], which had earlier recommended the passage of the Racial Justice Act, has called for a complete moratorium on executions until such problems can be adequately addressed. Other bar associations such as the Pennsylvania Bar, the Ohio Bar, the Chicago Council of Lawyers, the Massachusetts Bar and the Philadelphia Bar have either endorsed the ABA's resolution or passed similar resolutions. Over 100 other organizations have also endorsed motions to stop executions, at least until a greater sense of justice can be restored to the process.

Evidence of racial discrimination in the U.S. death penalty system has attracted worldwide attention. In 1996, the International Commission of Jurists, whose members include respected judges from around the world, visited the United States and researched the use of the death penalty. Their report was sharply critical of the way the death penalty is being applied, particularly in regards to race: "The Mission is of the opinion that . . . the administration of capital punishment in the United States continues to be discriminatory and unjust—and hence 'arbitrary'—, and thus not in consonance with Articles 6 and 14 of the Political Covenant and Article 2(c) of the Race Convention."

> *" The influence of race on the death penalty is pervasive and corrosive. "*

In a March, 1998 decision, the Inter-American Commission on Human Rights concluded that the U.S. had violated international law and should compensate the relatives of William Andrews, who was executed in Utah in 1992, because of racial bias in his case.

And most recently, the U.N. Special Rapporteur on Extraju-

dicial, Summary or Arbitrary Executions filed a report with the
U.N. Commission on Human Rights after his visit to the U.S.
stating that "race, ethnic origin and economic status appear to
be key determinants of who will, and will not, receive a sentence of death."

In Philadelphia, the Secretary General of Amnesty International criticized Pennsylvania's death penalty as "one of the
most racist and unfair in the U.S." Hours after his speech, the
Philadelphia Bar voted in favor of a resolution calling for a
moratorium on the death penalty in that state. The Governor's
office responded by pointing out that the only two persons
executed in Pennsylvania in recent times were both white.
However, these men were the exception, having been executed
before others only because they waived their appeals. The overwhelming majority of those on [the] state's death row are black,
and 84% of those on death row from Philadelphia are black.

Religious opposition to the death penalty has also cited the
racial unfairness in its application. Recently, all the Catholic
Bishops in Texas signed a statement calling for an end to the
death penalty, noting: "The imposition of the death penalty
has resulted in racial bias. In fact, the race of the victim has
proven to be the determining factor in deciding whether to
prosecute capital cases." Similar concerns have been voiced by
the National Conference of Catholic Bishops and the leaders of
other denominations.

The public in this country is very aware of the role race
plays in the death penalty. A recent poll by *Newsweek* magazine
revealed that about half of all Americans believe that a black
person is more likely to receive the death penalty than a white
person for the same crime. When such public reaction will result in a challenge to this injustice is not clear. Until then, it remains a serious source of division among the races and an em-
barrassment to the U.S.'s pursuit of international human rights.

We cannot ignore racial injustice

The influence of race on the death penalty is pervasive and cor-
rosive. In other areas of the law, protections have been built in
to limit the effects of systemic racism when the evidence of its
impact is clear. With the death penalty, however, such correc-
tive measures have been blocked by those who claim that capital punishment would bog down if racial fairness was required.
And so, the sore festers.

The new studies revealed through this report add to an overwhelming body of evidence that race plays a decisive role in the question of who lives and dies by execution in this country. Race influences which cases are chosen for capital prosecution and which prosecutors are allowed to make those decisions. Likewise, race affects the makeup of the juries which determine the sentence. Racial effects have been shown not just in isolated instances, but in virtually every state for which disparities have been estimated and over an extensive period of time.

Those who die because of this racism are not the kind of people who usually evoke the public's sympathy. Many have committed horrendous crimes. But crimes no less horrendous are committed by white offenders or against black victims, and yet the killers in those cases are generally spared death. The death penalty today is a system which vents society's anger over the problem of crime on a select few. The existing data clearly suggest that many of the death sentences are a product of racial discrimination. There is no way to maintain our avowed adherence to equal justice under the law, while ignoring such racial injustice in the state's taking of life.

9

The Execution of Juveniles in the United States Violates International Human Rights Law

Amnesty International USA

Amnesty International USA is the U.S. section of Amnesty International, an activist organization founded in 1961 to fight for human rights across the globe.

Despite the international view that it is unethical to put children to death for committing violent crimes, the United States continues to send people under the age of eighteen to death row. It is wrong to execute children who are not fully mature and therefore are not completely responsible for their actions. The execution of juveniles in the United States violates the human rights of children and should be stopped.

Fifty years after the [1948] adoption of the [United Nations] Universal Declaration of Human Rights, with its vision of universal freedom from state cruelty, more than half the countries of the world have abolished the death penalty in law or practice. Of the diminishing number of retentionist nations, the vast majority respect international human rights law by restricting capital punishment to adult offenders. It is ironic, then, that the country which repeatedly proclaims itself to be the world's most progressive force for human rights, in fact heads a tiny circle of nations with a far less distinguished claim to fame—the execution of people for crimes they committed as children.

The USA makes no secret of its determination to perpetrate this particular human rights violation. The federal government has explicitly reserved the right to defy the international ban on the use of the death penalty against those who commit crimes when under 18 years old, and state authorities pursue this practice apparently unconcerned about world opinion. As a result, some 70 juvenile offenders await their deaths at the hands of US officials. Eight such prisoners have been executed in the USA in the 1990s. In the same period, only five other countries—Iran, Nigeria, Pakistan, Saudi Arabia and Yemen—are known to have executed juvenile offenders, killing a total of nine such prisoners between them. . . .

> *How can this teach children to value life?*

As the rest of the world withdraws from using the death penalty against its children, some politicians in the USA are calling for their state legislatures to lower the age for capital defendants even below the current minimum of 16 set by the US Supreme Court.

Is this the action of a political leadership which "sees further into the future" than other countries, or one which still clings to one of the unacceptable practices from its past?

Wrong for all

About one in 50 of the more than 3,400 individuals on death row in the USA were convicted of crimes committed when they were under 18. As this report will illustrate, there are specific reasons, backed by an overwhelming international consensus, to oppose their death sentences. But it should not be forgotten that the use of the death penalty against *anyone* is a human rights violation of premeditated cruelty which denies the right to life proclaimed in the Universal Declaration of Human Rights. Stopping the execution of juvenile offenders, while being a major objective in itself, is just one step on the road to total abolition.

The cases of juvenile offenders on US death rows continue to reflect more than just the specific concerns raised by their youth at the time of the crime. They also illustrate the wider characteristics of a punishment whose time has passed: its inherent cruelty; its failure as a deterrent; its use against the mentally impaired; the risk of wrongful conviction; inadequate legal representation, particularly for poor defendants; and arbitrariness in sentencing as a result of politics, prejudice, and the power of state prosecutors to choose who will face a capital trial.

Those convicted and sentenced to death for crimes committed when they were under 18 are not the only children affected by the death penalty. Violent crime scars the young family members of its victims, but the brutal and brutalizing effects of the death penalty are also felt by children beyond death row. A child who has a family member executed becomes yet another victim in the cycle of violence; but all society's children, along with its adults, receive the message carried by the death penalty that killing is an effective and appropriate response to killing. How can this teach children to value life? . . .

Breaking consensus and the law

On 31 July 1998 Chief Justice Springer dissented from the majority opinion of the Supreme Court of Nevada when it confirmed the death sentence against Michael Domingues, convicted in 1994 for the murder of his next door neighbour and her four-year-old son in their home in Las Vegas in 1993. The crime took place when Michael Domingues was 16 years old. His appeal to the state Supreme Court had raised one issue: the illegality of his death sentence under international law.

There is now an almost global consensus that people who commit crimes when under 18 should not be subjected to the death penalty. This is not an attempt to excuse violent juvenile crime, or belittle the suffering of its victims and their families, but a recognition that children are not yet fully mature—hence not fully responsible for their actions—and that the possibilities for rehabilitation of a child or adolescent are greater than for adults. Indeed, international standards see the ban on the death penalty against people who were under 18 at the time of the offence to be such a fundamental safeguard that it may never be suspended, even in times of war or internal conflict. However, the US authorities seem to believe that juveniles in the USA are different from their counterparts in the rest of the world and should be denied this human right.

Principal among the human rights standards which seek to protect juvenile offenders from the death penalty, and the one cited in Michael Domingues' appeal, is Article 6(5) of the International Covenant on Civil and Political Rights (ICCPR), which states that "sentence of death shall not be imposed for crimes committed by persons below eighteen years of age. . .". The ICCPR came into force on 23 March 1976, coincidentally just a few weeks before the US Supreme Court ruled that US states could begin executing again under their new capital statutes. Executions resumed in January 1977. Since then, the number of crimes punishable by death and the number of executions have relentlessly increased in the USA, just as the list of countries which use the death penalty has been steadily shrinking. The USA has been even further out of step with the rest of the world as far as the death penalty for juvenile offenders is concerned.

The USA signed the ICCPR in October 1977—thereby binding itself not to do anything which would defeat the object and purpose of the treaty, pending a decision whether to ratify it. In the time between signature and eventual ratification in June 1992, the US authorities executed Charles Rumbaugh, James Terry Roach, Jay Pinkerton, Dalton Prejean and Johnny Garrett for crimes committed when they were 17. More than 70 juvenile offenders were sentenced to death during this period.

> *The USA has been even further out of step with the rest of the world as far as the death penalty for juvenile offenders is concerned.*

When it ratified the ICCPR, the US government made clear its intention to continue this practice by explicitly reserving the right to impose the death penalty for crimes committed by those under 18. Since ratification, the US authorities have put their words into lethal action six times against juvenile offenders, with the execution of Curtis Harris, Frederick Lashley, Ruben Cantu, Chris Burger, Joseph Cannon and Robert Carter. More than 50 juvenile offenders have been sent to death row during this period, including Michael Domingues. . . .

In Nevada on 31 July 1998, the state Supreme Court voted

that the US reservation to Article 6(5) of the ICCPR was valid and that the death sentence against Michael Domingues was legal. It reached this conclusion by looking to other US states rather than by examining international opinion or practice: *"Many of our sister jurisdictions have laws authorizing the death penalty for criminal offenders under the age of eighteen, and such laws have withstood Constitutional scrutiny."* It ignored the fact that a majority of US jurisdictions do *not* allow the death penalty to be used for crimes committed by under 18-year-olds, either because they have legislated to exempt such offenders from the death penalty, or because they do not allow it against anyone of any age. In 1998, 14 states and two federal jurisdictions (civilian and military) have legislation enforcing 18 as the minimum age, and 12 US states and the District of Columbia do not allow the death penalty at all. Twenty-four states allow for the use of the death penalty against those under 18, 15 of which had juvenile offenders on death row in June [1997]. . . .

Eighteen is the minimum age

A minimum age of 18 years at the time of the capital offence was established half a century ago. Article 68 of the Fourth Geneva Convention of 12 August 1949 Relative to the Protection of Civilian Persons in Time of War states that ". . . the death penalty may not be pronounced on a protected person who was under eighteen years of age at the time of the offence." When it ratified the Convention in 1955, the USA made no reservation to this particular paragraph. It has thus agreed for over four decades that, in the event of war or other armed conflict in which it may be involved, it will protect all civilian juvenile offenders in occupied countries from the death penalty. This is precisely the protection it refuses to offer children within its own borders in peacetime.

Since 1949 the ICCPR, CRC [Convention on the Rights of the Child] and various other international and regional human rights instruments have come into force setting 18 as the minimum age at which people can become eligible for the death penalty. In 1987 the Inter-American Commission on Human Rights declared that the USA had violated Article 1 of the American Declaration of the Rights and Duties of Man by executing two juvenile offenders, James Terry Roach and Jay Pinkerton. The Commission referred to the emerging principle of customary international law prohibiting such executions. In the 11 years since the ruling, the USA has executed eight more juvenile offenders, despite the fact that this "emerging" principle of customary international law has been even further strengthened by the almost global recognition of Article 37(a) of the CRC.

For any country to adopt a selective approach to its international human rights obligations can serve only to undermine respect for the system as a whole and to diminish the prospect for human rights for all. That the USA sentences to death and executes juvenile offenders in violation of international law should be a matter of deep concern to all inside and outside the country concerned with human progress. . . .

Cruel and unusual punishment

Rather than recognize the primacy of international law, as they should, the US authorities continue to look to the US Supreme Court, as interpreter of the Constitution, to set the minimum age at which people in the USA can become eligible for the death penalty. The Court has done this via the Constitution's Eighth Amendment, which bans "cruel and unusual punishments".

The Eighth Amendment was added to the US Constitution in 1791. In 1910 the Supreme Court stated that the Amendment *"is progressive and does not prohibit merely the cruel and unusual punishments known in 1689 and 1787, but may acquire wider meaning as public opinion becomes enlightened by humane justice."* In 1958 the Court took up this theme when it said that the definition of "cruel and unusual punishments" was not permanently fixed, but instead must draw its meaning from *"the evolving standards of decency that mark the progress of a maturing society."* In 1998 the Court's opinion of US "decency" is such that it continues to allow US authorities to sentence to death and execute juvenile offenders, in violation of international law.

> *It is time for US political leaders to . . . prohibit the use of the death penalty against* all *juvenile offenders.*

The Court made its ruling in 1989, when five of its nine Justices voted that the execution of offenders aged 16 or 17 at the time of their crimes did not violate the Eighth Amend-

ment. Justice Antonin Scalia, appointed by President Ronald
Reagan 18 months earlier, wrote for the majority opinion that
US society had not formed a consensus that the execution of
such offenders constituted cruel and unusual punishment. He
emphasized that the five reached their decision after looking to
US conceptions of decency—not the practice of other countries—in determining what constituted "evolving standards of
decency". The five determined that the death penalty against
16 and 17-year-olds was acceptable to US society because not
only did the laws of various states allow for its use against such
offenders, but juries and prosecutors applied those laws.

> *The goal of retribution . . . cannot be achieved by killing someone who may not have been fully responsible for their actions.*

Amnesty International believes that the Court was wrong to
have relied on this "objective evidence" to set a rule of constitutional law, as well as being wrong to have ignored universal
"standards of decency" reflected in international human rights
instruments. For it presupposed a society fully informed about
the death penalty, and a capital justice system fully representa-
tive of society's views in which the decision-making of legislators, prosecutors and juries was free from prejudice and politics.
However, the death penalty in the USA is, as it was in 1989, a
politicized punishment, used disproportionately against racial
and ethnic minorities and the poor; the debate over its use
takes place in a highly-charged and emotional climate of opinion, with large parts of US society ill-informed about its effectiveness and alternatives, or their country's international obligations. In the case of juvenile offenders, many have been
sentenced to death by juries which were not in a position to
fully consider the mitigating aspects of the youth and backgrounds of the defendants. Also the Supreme Court ignored the
fact that a majority of states did not allow the death penalty to
be used against those under 18 at the time of the offence. All
these factors render the basis of the Court's ruling as unreliable
as if it had looked to public opinion polls. It had rejected the
latter as "too uncertain a foundation" for matters of constitutional law. . . .

In 1996 the International Commission of Jurists reported on the US death penalty. It noted that the USA's ratification of international standards such as the ICCPR represents "an important milestone in the progress of a maturing US society", and means that US authorities must no longer confine their definition of "standards of decency" to national criteria and opinion. Instead they must look to global standards, as articulated by international human rights instruments.

Human rights have no borders. The Universal Declaration of Human Rights spoke of the universal dimension of humanity when it recognized that "the inherent dignity and the equal and inalienable rights of all members of the human family is the foundation of freedom, justice and peace in the world". [More than] fifty years [later], it is time for the USA to take a fresh look at what constitutes "standards of decency" today, and to redefine the Eighth Amendment ban on "cruel and unusual punishments" in line with international standards. Nearly 90 years have passed since the US Supreme Court said that the amendment was *"not fastened to the obsolete, but may acquire meaning as public opinion becomes more enlightened."* It is 40 years since the Court noted that *"if the word 'unusual' is to have any meaning apart from the word 'cruel'. . . the meaning should be the ordinary one, signifying something different from that which is generally done."* At the end of the 1990s, the use of the death penalty against juvenile offenders is so unusual as to be almost unknown outside of the USA. Its *cruelty* against anyone is undeniable.

It is time for US political leaders to loosen their grip on "the obsolete" and prohibit the use of the death penalty against *all* juvenile offenders, as defined by international standards, as a first step towards total abolition. . . .

Why protect violent children?

Defence lawyer Beth Davis was pleading for the life of DeShun Washington at the sentencing phase of his trial in Missouri on 31 August 1998. The jury had found him guilty of first-degree murder two days earlier. DeShun Washington was 16 at the time of the crime.

Thirty-five years ago, US Supreme Court Justice Frankfurter observed that *"children have a very special place in life which law should reflect."* Today this universal truth has been reflected in the almost worldwide acceptance of the principle that juvenile offenders should be excluded from the death penalty. The need to consider the "best interests of the child", as expressed by Article 3 of the Convention on the Rights of the Child, can never be fulfilled by sending juvenile offenders to death row or killing them.

Within the USA, as elsewhere, there has been long-standing and widespread recognition that children are different in the eyes of the law. For example, a Presidential Commission reporting on youth crime in the 1970s observed that *"[c]rimes committed by youths may be just as harmful to victims as those committed by older persons, but they deserve less punishment because adolescents may have less capacity to control their conduct and to think in long-range terms than adults. Moreover, youth crime as such is not exclusively the offender's fault; offenses by the young also represent a failure of family, school, and the social system, which share responsibility for the development of America's youth."* On average, it costs some two and a half million US dollars to prosecute, keep on death row and execute a single individual. Surely this money, not to mention the human energy involved, could be put to better use in preventive efforts to remedy the sorts of failure referred to by the Commission.

> *There is an overwhelming international legal and moral consensus against any nation executing juvenile offenders.*

In the early 1980s, the Section of Criminal Justice of the American Bar Association (ABA) conducted a two-year study which concluded that the death penalty was an inappropriate punishment for juvenile offenders and that *"the spectacle of our society seeking legal vengeance through the execution of a child should not be countenanced. . .".* In 1983, the ABA adopted a resolution opposing "the imposition of capital punishment upon any person for an offense committed while under the age of 18." This was the first time that the ABA had taken a position on any aspect of the death penalty. In 1997, it reiterated its outright opposition to the execution of juvenile offenders when it called for a moratorium on the death penalty in the USA. . . .

It is commonly agreed that the death penalty's would-be goals of either retribution or deterrence are especially inapplicable in the case of young people. In 1989, citing the findings of the report by its Section on Criminal Justice, the ABA said *". . . in light of the characteristics associated with childhood—impulsiveness, lack of self control, poor judgement, feelings of invincibility—the deterrent value of the juvenile death penalty is likely of little consequence. . .".*

The goal of retribution, which presupposes exact like-for-like punishment, cannot be achieved by killing someone who may not have been fully responsible for their actions. In *Thompson v. Oklahoma* [1988], the US Supreme Court stated that *"given the lesser culpability of the juvenile offender, the teenager's capacity for growth, and society's fiduciary* [protective] *obligations to its children"* the goal of retribution is inapplicable to the execution of 15-year-old offenders. Its refusal to apply this ruling to 16 and 17-year-olds contravenes the principle that the state should assume the role of protector for all its children and youth. Politicians who call for younger children to be eligible for the death penalty are putting pressure on the state to absolve itself even further from its protective role. . . .

A step in the "rights" direction

In the USA and many other countries, violent crime is a serious problem. Such crimes have tragic and lasting ramifications for the families and loved ones of the victims. As an organization dedicated to the victims of human rights violations, Amnesty International would never seek to excuse or belittle these crimes. But the death penalty is a calculated denial of the right to life and the right not to be subjected to cruel, inhuman or degrading punishment, basic rights to which all human beings are entitled, no matter who they are or what they have done.

The current use of the death penalty in the USA is driven by anger and fear about violent crime, desire for retributive justice, and by elected officials unwilling to risk their careers by supporting alternatives. Fear of violent crime, whether juvenile or adult, can make many citizens feel that abandoning the death penalty would be a leap into the dark. Yet it is no longer a step into the unknown; the experience of very many countries has shown that there are alternatives to the death penalty and that there is no descent into social disorder following abolition. For example, the murder rate in Canada dropped by 34 per cent in the 20 years that followed abolition in 1976.

There is an overwhelming international legal and moral consensus against any nation executing juvenile offenders. However heinous the crime, the sentencing to death and execution of a young person denies the possibility of rehabilitation, cannot be justified on grounds of retribution or deterrence, and is contrary to contemporary standards of justice and humane treatment in every corner of the world. As the world marks 50 years of the Universal Declaration of Human Rights, ending the death penalty against juvenile offenders would be a particularly appropriate step for the US government to take towards total abolition and towards meeting its promise of rights for all.

Amnesty International urges the US government to take this step now.

10

Capital Punishment of the Mentally Disabled Requires Special Consideration

Douglas Mossman

Douglas Mossman is professor and director of forensic psychiatry at the Wright State University School of Medicine. He is also an adjunct professor at the University of Dayton School of Law.

In the late 1980s, the Supreme Court ruled that executing mentally retarded murderers is constitutional. In 2002, however, the Supreme Court reversed its decision, deeming such executions "cruel and unusual." Although this decision may seem like a victory for death penalty opponents, in fact it threatens to make the legal system even more arbitrary and capricious than before. The main problem is that the criteria for diagnosing mental retardation are extremely imprecise. In addition, it is discriminatory to make blanket decisions about individuals, including judgments about their moral capacity, on the basis of a mental disability.

In the late 1980s, the Supreme Court was asked whether mental retardation should exempt a murderer from the death penalty. In *Penry v. Lynaugh*, a majority answered that it should not. The Court did say that letting jurors consider expert testimony about retardation and childhood abuse was crucial to a "reasoned moral response" about whether to impose a death sentence. But since at the time only two states prohibited the execution of mentally retarded persons, the Court concluded there was not "sufficient evidence at present of a national consensus" that executing such persons would be "cruel and unusual punishment."

Now, however, the Supreme Court has changed its mind. In *Atkins v. Virginia*, decided in June 2002, a majority of justices concluded that a "national consensus" had been reached in opposition to executing mentally retarded persons, and thus doing so would henceforth be unconstitutional. A practice that the Court found acceptable in 1989 had become "cruel and unusual punishment" 13 years later.

The Atkins decision has been attacked by strict constructionists—in his dissent Justice [Antonin] Scalia called it "nothing but the personal views of its members"—and by supporters of the death penalty. But death penalty opponents should also be wary of a decision that threatens to add more confusion and arbitrariness to an already capricious system and that seriously distorts the use of psychiatric diagnosis. To see why, one needs to consider the specifics of Daryl Renard Atkins' case, the Supreme Court majority's statements about his mental condition and diagnosis, the potential impact of these statements on the testimony of mental health experts, and the consequences for future sentencing determinations in death penalty cases.

Prelude to murder

Though Daryl Atkins was still a teenager when he committed murder, his intellectual limitations and social maladjustment had already been evident for years. Documents prepared by defense lawyers report that Atkins flunked and repeated second grade and received mainly Ds and Fs through seventh grade. School officials finally referred him for special-education testing, but he never was evaluated. He received all Fs in eighth grade, and despite not meeting requirements for entering high school, he was placed in the ninth grade, where he continued to perform poorly. He did better once he was placed in classes for "slow learners," but he still left school without graduating. By age 18—the age at which he was arrested for the murder of Eric Nesbitt—Atkins had not learned how to do laundry or cook meals for himself.

Atkins' serious behavioral problems began in early adolescence. At age 13, he was convicted of breaking-and-entering and petty larceny, and in eighth grade he started abusing drugs. At age 17, he was convicted of two counts of grand larceny. Several months before Nesbitt's murder, Atkins participated in two armed robberies; during one of these, he hit the victim on the head with a bottle. Two weeks before the murder, Atkins attacked a woman and shot her in the stomach.

At around midnight on August 16, 1996, having spent the day drinking alcohol and smoking marijuana, Atkins and William Jones drove to a 7-11 store, intending to rob a customer. Eric Nesbitt, an airman from Langley Air Force Base, became their victim. After robbing Nesbitt at gunpoint, they took him to a nearby ATM and forced him to withdraw $200. They then drove to a deserted area and shot him eight times. A videotape of the ATM transaction allowed police to identify and locate the two men.

Verdict in the courts

At Atkins' trial, each man claimed the other had shot and killed Nesbitt, but Jones's testimony was considered more believable, and the jury convicted Atkins of capital murder. During the trial's penalty phase, jurors heard about Atkins' previous criminal activity. The defense responded with one witness, a psychologist who testified about his interviews of people who knew Atkins, his examination of school and court records, and the results of an IQ test he had administered, on which Atkins scored only 59. Despite the psychologist's testimony that Atkins was "mildly mentally retarded" and would not pose a threat to others in prison, two Virginia juries sentenced Atkins to death. (A second sentencing hearing was held because the original trial court had used a misleading verdict form.)

When Atkins' lawyers appealed the death sentence, they did not claim that execution would be disproportionate to penalties imposed for similar crimes in Virginia. Rather, they argued that Atkins should not be sentenced to death because he was mentally retarded. A majority of the Virginia Supreme Court rejected this argument, relying on the U.S. Supreme Court's 1989 ruling in Penry, which stated that mental retardation could be a mitigating factor but not an absolute barrier to capital punishment. Two state supreme court justices disagreed, however, arguing that retarded persons are "less culpable for their criminal acts" than other offenders because they "have substantial limitations not shared by the general population. A moral and civilized society diminishes itself if its system of justice does not afford recognition and consideration of those limitations in a meaningful way."

Impressed by "the gravity of the concerns expressed" in the state supreme court's dissenting opinion, the U.S. Supreme Court agreed to hear Atkins' case and to revisit their 1989 decision in Penry. Between 1989 and 2002, the number of states with laws barring death sentences for mentally retarded persons had grown from two to eighteen, and legislatures in three other states had taken steps toward adopting such laws. Writing for the Supreme Court majority, Justice [John Paul] Stevens concluded that the passage of so many laws since the Penry decision showed that "much has changed" in the public's attitude about executing retarded persons. This "national consensus," which reflected "the evolving standards of decency that mark the progress of a maturing society," required the Court to change the stance it had adopted just 13 years earlier. Henceforth, a diagnosis of mental retardation would spare any murderer from the death penalty.

Criteria for diagnosis

Footnotes in Atkins quote at length from diagnostic criteria that psychiatric organizations have developed to identify people with mental retardation. For example, the current diagnostic manual of the American Psychiatric Association (APA) describes mental retardation as

> significantly subaverage general intellectual functioning . . . accompanied by significant limitations in adaptive functioning in at least two of the following skill areas: communication, self-care, home living, social/interpersonal skills, use of community resources, self-direction, functional academic skills, work, leisure, health, and safety . . . [with] onset . . . before age 18 years.

Referring to such criteria, Justice Stevens argued that "by definition," persons with mental retardation "have diminished capacities to understand and process information, to communicate, to abstract from mistakes and learn from experience, to engage in logical reasoning, to control impulses, and to understand the reactions of others." Although retarded criminals may know right from wrong, their mental deficiencies "diminish their personal culpability. Thus, pursuant to our narrowing jurisprudence, which seeks to ensure that only the most deserving of execution are put to death, an exclusion for the mentally retarded is appropriate."

> *// Making psychiatric diagnosis the basis for a life-or-death legal decision would cause no scientific or practical problems. //*

Mental health professionals have generally praised the Atkins decision. The APA and the American Association on Mental Retardation (AAMR) were among the many mental health organizations that had signed on to friend-of-the-court briefs urging the Supreme Court to ban executions of retarded persons. When the Atkins decision was announced, Doree'n Croser, AAMR's executive director, was "deeply grateful" that the Supreme Court had stopped "this barbaric practice of killing persons who do not have the full intellectual capacity to understand the crime they committed. . . . This is an important day for disability advocates and for our country." Renee Binder, chair of the APA's Committee on Judicial Action, praised the decision "because it recognizes that there are objective and reliable determinations of whether an individual has mental retardation when the assessment is done by qualified professionals with substantial experience."

Binder's comment echoes points emphasized in the friend-of-the-court brief that the APA (along with the American Psychological Association and the American Academy of Psychiatry and Law) had filed with the Supreme Court. The brief argued that making psychiatric diagnosis the basis for a life-or-death legal decision would cause no scientific or practical problems. Both "incorrect diagnoses" and "unnecessary legal wrangling" could be avoided "because mental retardation can be identified using time-tested instruments and protocols with proven validity and reliability." To diagnose a person as having mental retardation, professionals must find that "three necessary criteria are all present: significant limitations in intellectual functioning, significant limitations in practical or adaptive functioning, and onset before adulthood." Psychologists and psychiatrists can make "an objective determination" about whether the accused suffers from mental retardation using established measures of intelligence and adaptive functioning, so that clinicians "undertaking separate assessments should reach the same conclusion." Yet to anyone knowledgeable about mental retardation and the methods used to diagnose it, this assertion is remarkable.

Are all mentally retarded persons alike?

The "by definition" language of the Atkins decision suggests that persons with mental retardation form a group who are clearly distinct from nonretarded persons. In reality, mental retardation is an artificial category imposed on a spectrum of human capability. The diagnostic line that separates persons with mental retardation from those who are only well below average is a changing and arbitrary one.

One reason for this is that the criteria defining mental retardation, like most diagnostic criteria used by mental health professionals, often get revised. Over the past century, the AAMR has "updated" its definition of mental retardation 10 times. The most recent changes were published five days before the Atkins decision, in the tenth edition of the AAMR's official classification manual. Although psychiatric diagnoses are often revised to reflect new understandings, scientific breakthroughs, or the availability of new treatments, politics can play a role. An AAMR advertisement for Mental Retardation: Definition, Classification and Systems of Supports states unabashedly that the 2002 edition

> proposes a state-of-the-art method to define, classify, and support an individual with mental retardation. In view of the recent U.S. Supreme Court decision to ban execution of persons with mental retardation, the 10th edition is a timely and critical resource to the states as they strive to come up with a current and fuller definition of mental retardation.

The AAMR currently defines mental retardation as "a disability characterized by significant limitations both in intellectual functioning and in adaptive behavior as expressed in conceptual, social, and practical adaptive skills. This disability originates before the age of 18." This characterization appears reasonably close to the previously quoted definition used by the APA. Beyond this point, however, the two professional organizations begin to part in their definitions. The APA's diagnostic manual categorizes mental retardation according to its overall severity—that is, as either mild, moderate, severe, or profound. Since 1992, however, the AAMR has specifically rejected this approach. Instead, it encourages diagnosticians to examine patterns of limitations in a person's everyday functioning, and to describe the degree of support those persons need, which may be "intermittent," "limited," "extensive," or "pervasive."

If persons with mental retardation were members of a homogeneous, discrete biological or psychological category of persons, readily distinguishable from persons without mental retardation, professional organizations might have an easier time settling on clinical criteria for diagnosing the condition. There are retarded persons whose impairments make them easily identifiable: They have severe academic problems during childhood, limited communication skills, and need, even as adults, to be supervised at work or where they live. But such individuals make up only 15 percent of all retarded persons. Mildly retarded persons, who comprise the remaining 85 percent, usually develop social and work skills that enable them to minimally support themselves, though they need guidance in making complicated decisions.

> *The manuals have aimed not to categorize people, but to categorize their mental disorders.*

The medical conditions that can cause intellectual impairment are countless. They include chromosomal defects, biochemical abnormalities, and infections that alter the brain's development before birth or during early childhood. In many cases of mild mental retardation, though, no specific medical reason for the person's limitations can be identified. Clinicians thus cannot use biological tests to decide whether a person is mentally retarded.

Instead, persons with mental retardation are generally identified through tests of intelligence and social capabilities administered by specially trained professionals. When the intellectual capabilities of a large, randomly selected group of persons are measured by such tests, the result is what statisticians call a "normal distribution," often described as a "bell curve." At one end of the distribution lie geniuses, and on the other end are profoundly impaired persons; bright, average, and dull folks make up the vast majority in the middle. Intelligence testing produces a numerical result—an "intelligence quotient" or IQ score—that allows psychologists to place an individual along the spectrum of cognitive ability. Other, lesser-known tests enable psychologists and mental retardation specialists to rank individuals in terms of "adaptive" capabilities—such as communication abilities, work skills, and caring for oneself—for which the population as a whole is also continuously distributed.

IQ scores are set up so that the "mean" or average score is 100, and the "standard deviation" is 15. Approximately 95 percent of a normally distributed population lies within two standard deviations of the mean, and individuals lying outside this arbitrary statistical boundary are often deemed "abnormal." A cut-off IQ score of 70—two standard deviations below the mean score of 100—has been set as the intelligence level that separates persons with mental retardation from persons whom mental health professionals designate as having "borderline intellectual functioning." Yet such numerical definitions of mental retardation, with all the apparent precision of a mathematical formula, belie the inherent subjectivity and complexity of the problem.

Life or death decisions

When conscientious mental health professionals interpret IQ scores and plan treatment interventions, they keep in mind that someone who scores 69 on an IQ test is practically indistinguishable from someone who scores 71, and that two persons with IQ scores of 67 and 73 have much more in common with each other than with a person who scores 88. If existing state statutes are any guide, however, legislatures and courts may lose sight of these facts when they put Atkins into practice. Of the 18 state statutes in effect when Atkins was decided, 11 made specific IQ scores part of the criteria for exempting a defendant from the death penalty. In other words, some statutes that implement Atkins-type barriers against execution are written such that a one-point change in a person's IQ score could make a life-or-death difference.

The availability of IQ test scores suggests that mental health professionals can offer courts objective, precise methods for deciding who is so impaired that the death penalty should be ruled out. Yet in truth the numbers that IQ tests generate are far from perfectly reliable measurements of a person's cognitive ability. Under the best conditions, IQ tests have a "measurement error" of about five points. An individual who scores, say, 68 on one administration has a 95 percent chance of scoring between 63 and 73 on subsequent administrations. More than half of the persons whose IQ results fall in the mildly retarded range receive scores of 65 to 70—that is, their scores' margin of error will include 70.

> **❝** *The APA has vigorously endorsed the Americans With Disabilities Act (ADA), which provides broad protections against discrimination based on mental or physical disabilities.* **❞**

Additional uncertainty arises because, for many items, the test administrator has to decide how many points a subject's response deserves. In normal clinical use, these ambiguities do not matter a great deal. But in testing a defendant for whom a one- or two-point change in IQ score has life-and-death implications, clinicians may have a hard time being objective in interpreting a response. The net result of all these imperfections is that judges or juries will often find it difficult to decide which side of the arbitrary line—between mentally retarded and merely "dull"—a defendant falls.

Compounding these problems is the fact that Atkins leaves state legislatures considerable room to make mischief. Although the Atkins majority found that persons with mental retardation are "by definition" less culpable, the opinion also specifically leaves the task of codifying criteria for mental retardation to the state legislatures. In many states with pre-Atkins statutes, specific IQ scores either are required for a diagnosis of mental retardation or constitute presumptive evidence for or against that diagnosis; such laws give results of a single administration of an intelligence test far more weight than mental health professionals believe is warranted. In most cases, statutes use a score of 70 as the cut-off point, but sometimes other scores—65 or 75, for example—are used for key decisions.

Nothing in Atkins requires states to follow the diagnostic criteria used by mental health professionals. States could presumably adopt differing IQ scores and introduce procedural variations when they draft statutes implementing the Atkins decision, even though this would let some states execute persons whom the laws of other states would exempt from the death penalty.

Categorizing the mentally retarded

The APA's support of the Atkins decision is all the more remarkable in view of organized psychiatry's longstanding opposition to using diagnostic categories for legal and social purposes. In a 1996 friend-of-the-court brief filed in *Kansas v. Hendricks*—a Supreme Court case concerning post-prison confinement of sex offenders—the APA explained why legal decisions should not be determined by categories derived from a medical diagnostic scheme.

The classification schemes are developed and periodically altered, through comprehensive field trials, research, and analysis, to serve diagnostic and statistical functions, forming a common (and always imperfect) language for gathering clinical data and for communication among mental health professionals. . . . Such comprehensive classification schemes are not . . . designed to identify those [persons who are] subject to various legal standards. . . . Not all individuals who come within a [diagnostic] category suffer an impairment that diminishes their autonomy.

In recent decades, each edition of the APA's diagnostic manual has included a "Cautionary Statement" stating that its purpose

> is to provide clear descriptions of diagnostic categories in order to enable clinicians and investigators to diagnose, communicate about, study, and treat people with various mental disorders. . . . The clinical and scientific considerations involved in categorization of these conditions as mental disorders may not be wholly relevant to legal judgments, for example, that take into account such issues as individual responsibility.

The APA's diagnostic manuals also have emphasized the limitations of the diagnostic schemes they exemplify. The manuals have aimed not to categorize people, but to categorize their mental disorders. Therefore, it is incorrect to conclude that all individuals who are diagnosed with a particular disorder "are alike in all important ways," the manual explains. "Individuals sharing a diagnosis are likely to be heterogeneous even in regard to the defining features of the[ir] diagnosis and . . . boundary cases will be difficult to diagnose in any but a probabilistic fashion." Noting that the "imperfect fit" between legal and medical categories poses "risks" and "dangers" of misusing diagnoses, the current manual warns (as did its predecessor) that, when deciding whether a person meets a particular legal standard of responsibility, "additional information is usually required beyond that contained" in the diagnostic manual's description of a mental disorder. In other words, until Atkins, the APA consistently opposed equating moral and legal status with psychiatric diagnosis.

Causes for concern

Since its enactment in July 1990, the APA has vigorously endorsed the Americans With Disabilities Act (ADA), which provides broad protections against discrimination based on mental or physical disabilities. The APA's position is consistent with its longstanding wish to reduce the stigma associated with having a mental disorder. In a 1997 position statement, the APA criticized the use of psychiatric diagnoses in making decisions regarding employment, insurance, housing, or credit, because such thinking often reflects widespread but baseless beliefs about mental conditions. Indeed, said the APA:

> categorical distinctions based on mental disorder are tantamount to class discrimination because they assume that everyone who has received a particular diagnosis or treatment is identical. In fact, individuals with the same diagnosis . . . may manifest different kinds of symptoms; even when the symptoms are the same, they may vary widely in their severity. Nor is there a direct or simple connection between symptoms severity and impairments that may be relevant to a particular decision.

In many contexts, making blanket decisions about individuals on the basis of a mental disability—for example, denying them jobs, accommodations, or public services out of a belief that their disability makes them less responsible—has become illegal since the passage of the ADA. Yet the Supreme Court majority in the Atkins case makes exactly this kind of "categorical distinction," stating explicitly that all persons diagnosed with mental retardation necessarily lack the capacity to accept full moral responsibility for their actions. Justice Scalia made this very point in his dissent: "The Court concludes that no one who is even slightly mentally retarded can have sufficient moral responsibility to be subjected to capital punishment for any crime. As a sociological and moral conclusion that is implausible."

An approach more consistent with that mandated by the ADA and (usually) advocated by mental health professionals would be to allow an individualized decision about each defendant, one that would take into account his mental condition but not allow it to determine his moral capacity. This was what the Supreme Court's Penry decision recommended, and what the jurors who condemned Atkins did. After jurors heard ample testimony about his mental retardation, they concluded, as Justice Scalia put it, that Atkins' condition "was not a compelling reason to exempt him from the death penalty in light of the brutality of his crime and his long demonstrated propensity for violence."

11

It Is Unethical for Health Care Workers to Participate in Executions

Dave Holmes and Cary Federman

Dave Holmes is an assistant professor at the University of Ottawa's School of Nursing, as well as a nurse-researcher at the Douglas Hospital Research Centre in Montreal, Canada. He has published articles about the field of nursing in Nursing Inquiry, Journal of Psychosocial Nursing, *and* Punishment and Society. *Cary Federman is an assistant professor in Duquesne University's political science department.*

Since health care professionals normally act to save lives, their participation in executions is disturbing. States that employ heath care professionals to assist in executions are attempting to give the grim proceedings an aura of humanitarianism. In creating such a calm and clinical atmosphere, states are trying to quell objections to the death penalty.

The American rhetoric regarding human rights is internationally known and witnessed. Though describing itself as the benchmark of freedom and human rights, the United States of America violates several United Nations motions, and thus international conventions and laws, regarding human rights. The death penalty in the United States of America constitutes one of the most blatant of these many violations. According to Amnesty International, the death penalty is the ultimate denial of human rights because it violates the right to life.

Dave Holmes and Cary Federman, "Killing for the State: The Darkest Side of American Nursing," *Nursing Inquiry*, vol. 10, 2003, pp. 2–10. Copyright © 2003 by Blackwell Publishing, Ltd. All rights reserved. Reproduced by permission of Blackwell Publishers.

The United States leads the world in executions

More than half of the countries in the world now forbid the
death penalty. Yet, the United States has accelerated the rate of
executing condemned inmates. Six people each month are executed in the US, more than 800 since 1976 (as of 1 December
2002) and 3500 are on deathrow waiting to die, some, for years.
The United States, along with other so-called human rights vi-
olators, as classified by the US State Department (such as: Af-
ghanistan, Bangladesh, Chad, China, Iran, Iraq, North Korea,
Libya, Malaysia, Nigeria, Pakistan, Saudi Arabia, Sudan and
Yemen), continues to use capital punishment. While some
techniques used by certain states are seen as barbaric (behead-
ing, crucifixion, stoning), some are considered 'more humane'
(electrocution, hanging, lethal injection).

Over 85% of executions recorded by Amnesty International
occurred in the United States, China and Saudi Arabia. Of juvenile offenders executed, the United States executed half of
them; Yemen, Nigeria, Saudi Arabia, Pakistan and Iran the other
half. Having said that, the 'apparatus' of capital punishment in
the United States relies on several agents in order to fulfill its
deathwork.

Unethical role for healthcare workers

The aim of this article is to bring to the attention of the international nursing community the discrepancy between a pervasive 'caring' nursing discourse and a most unethical nursing
practice in the United States. In considering the important role
healthcare providers, namely nurses and physicians, play in administering death to the condemned (whether through care
during the deathrow period, finding veins for lethal injections
or checking for vital signs of life after the execution), we assert
that nurses and physicians are part of the states' penal machinery in America. Healthcare professionals who take part in
execution protocols are state functionaries who approach the
condemned body as angels of death. As such, they constitute
an extension of the state which exercises its sovereign power
over captive prisoners. . . .

The relationship between nurses and inmates

By replacing the electric chair with a gurney and a hooded executioner with a nurse or a physician, lethal injections offer the

spectacle of calm. As [Robert] Johnson has written, 'Executions today are disturbingly, even chillingly, dispassionate'. For some, it constitutes an improvement in the management of capital punishment.

[According to scholars Cary Federman and Dave Holmes:]

> Lethal injections offer the promise of a humanitarian solution to a criminal act, the cure for an ill, rather than the threat of societal retribution or punishment. Their appeal lies not in reducing pain to the prisoner, but in imposing a 'medical veneer' to the act of killing. By minimizing resistance, the procedures of control are more total. . . .

The move toward lethal injections was not motivated solely by humanitarian sentiment but rather by [according to Jonathan Abernathy] 'a desire on the part of legislators to neutralize public opposition to the death penalty after *Gregg v. Georgia*.'[1] The development of the 'long drop', for example, made hangings more efficient and less painful, and also helped to insulate Washington state's capital punishment statute from constitutional attack. Economics also plays a role. The state of Texas lists the cost of a lethal injection at $86.08; Florida, by contrast, which uses the electric chair, pays the person who throws the switch $150.00.

Focusing on the general public's reaction directs attention away from the healthcare profession's involvement with the prisoner and his confinement, a relationship that is not only hidden from public view, but is also legally protected. Consequently, we regard the state's interest in the way capital punishment is practiced in more insular terms, as the creation of autonomous state actors searching for economical and scientific ways to kill prisoners, perhaps in part, to reduce pain, but overall to serve particular ends of control and regulation, and to fulfill the state's idea of punishment as civilized. . . .

The death penalty as state apparatus

The need for lethal injections is less in the interest of the public than of the state. The invention of the penitentiary and the use of capital punishment in the United States are more than the 'byproducts of the intellectual and humanitarian move-

1. the court case that reinstated the death penalty

ments of the eighteenth century that contributed so generously to the founding of the American nation' [according to historian Blake McKelvey]. Taken together, the penitentiary and capital punishment in the US constitute a unified (but partial) story in the development of the state. Rejecting the prison as a history of good intentions, we regard the emergence of the penitentiary as 'constitutive of liberal democracy' [in the words of scholar Thomas Dumm]. Jails, penitentiaries, and prisons are the creations of autonomous state agents and intellectuals using the available scientific and technological knowledge concerning death, control, and discipline to further dispossess prisoners, isolate them from the public, and transform them. . . .

> *Healthcare professionals who take part in execution protocols . . . approach the condemned body as angels of death.*

In dealing with the role of science (knowledge) in politics, particularly in the execution process, we are less concerned with knowledge 'for what?' than with knowledge 'about what?'. That is, we are not trying to understand the instrumental purpose of using nursing and medical knowledges to hasten death, for its purpose is clear. In liberal democracies such as the United States, 'where knowledge is produced in an ethos of free competition' [writes scholar S. Scheingold], state actors need knowledge about more humane methods of putting criminals to death to alleviate any potential public outcry about the degree or excessiveness of punishment. Thus, although it is quite possible that lethal injections are as painful as electrocutions, and [according to Fordham University law professor Deborah Denno] the 'procedure becomes more . . . problematic for the untrained executioner', support for the procedure is high because of its perceived humanitarianism. As [social psychologist Phoebe] Ellsworth and [University of Michigan law professor Samuel] Gross point out, Americans support the death penalty more out of moral concerns and prejudice than as a method of control.

In the realm of penology, politics needs science and healthcare practitioners to substitute the more repressive methods of punishment and control with more palatable techniques (and persons) because of the finality of punishment and its effect on modern sensibilities. Yet what is missing in most surveys of the execution process is insight into the multiple meanings and applications of the practitioners of science with the practitioners of politics when they converge around a gurney.

Medicalized penal procedures remove the state from the language, if not the realm, of punishment. After witnessing the first electrical execution in New York in 1890, Dr Alfred Southwick, the inventor of the electric chair, said, 'We live in a higher civilization from this day'. This kind of language is not uncommon among American penal reformers. Since the Enlightenment, the advance of social knowledge and the strengthening of the state have been linked by [what professors Dietrich Rueschemeyer and Theda Skocpol call] 'a compelling vision of progress.' As the Supreme Court has noted, the replacement of hanging with electrocution 'did not increase the punishment of murder, but only changed its mode'. Death by lethal injection is an extension of, and not a replacement for, death by electrocution. More than denoting a new fusion of technology and state power, medicalized penal procedures represent a new configuration in the relationship among the state, its agents, and those in custody. . . .

Special protection for healthcare workers

Nursing and medical sciences are represented in prison by the presence of trained personnel who operate the machines and demonstrate the professional techniques used to carry the lethal solutions to the body of the condemned. South Dakota's capital punishment statute states that:

> An execution carried out by lethal injection shall be performed by a person selected by the warden and trained to administer the injection. The person administering the injection need not be a physician, registered nurse or licensed practical nurse or registered under the law of this or any other state.

Various states indemnify the healthcare personnel involved in executing prisoners. The South Dakota statute states that 'Any infliction of the punishment of death by administration of the required lethal substance or substances in the manner required by this section may not be construed to be the practice of medicine'. The South Dakota statute denies that there is an ethical (or legal) problem in procuring healthcare professionals to insert tubes into prisoners or to obtain the medicine (*Heckler v. Chaney* 1985) used to extinguish life. Idaho's capital punishment statute is no different:

> any infliction of the punishment of death by administration of the required lethal substance or substances in the manner required by this section shall not be construed to be the practice of medicine and any pharmacist or pharmaceutical supplier is authorized to dispense drugs to the director or his designee, without prescription, for carrying out the provisions of this section, notwithstanding any other provision of law.

Kansas's death penalty statute gives the secretary of corrections full power to control the death process. The secretary 'shall designate one or more executioners' to carry out the lethal injection in a 'swift and humane manner'. The secretary's discretion, however, is circumscribed by a legal requirement to 'appoint a panel of three persons to advise the secretary' on the 'type of substance or substances to be administered' to the condemned prisoner. The Kansas penal authority requires scientific knowledge to exercise its power over the condemned.

As an important part of the execution apparatus, healthcare professionals constitute a new and critical element of social control in prison. The laws, however, hide their importance, as if to point out that the prisoner, not the doctor, is the subject of inquiry. . . .

The state exploits healthcare workers

The state appropriates the nurse's and physician's knowledge, using them like prison labor force. Others practice their craft, use their methodologies, evoke the symbols of their trade. But she/he cannot be named and her/his role is unclear. Is she/he or isn't she/he the executioner? It is as if the laws can only recognize one subject—the convicted. Everyone else is a spectator.

Healthcare professionals are necessary for modern-day executions because of their status as scientists and caregivers. Idaho's capital punishment statute denies that administering lethal injections constitutes the practice of medicine, and protects against 'unnecessary suffering' of the condemned by using 'expert technical assistance'. If Idaho's director of the department of corrections cannot obtain expert technical assistance to carry out the lethal injection, the method of execution switches to firing squad. Idaho equates less scientific methods of execution with less humane forms of execution. Utah's death statute separates execution by 'shooting', which is carried out by a 'five-person firing squad of peace officers', and death by lethal injection, which is carried out by 'two or more persons trained in accordance with accepted medical practices'.

> *// Medicalized penal procedures remove the state from the language, if not the realm, of punishment. //*

'Expert technical assistance' over life and death is so important that law must protect that status, regardless of who is dispensing knowledge and exercising power. Montana's execution statute allows any person trained by the warden to administer death. 'The person administering the injection need not be a physician, registered nurse, or licensed practical nurse licensed or registered under the laws of this or any other state' [according to the statute]. Yet the 'identity of the executioner must remain anonymous. Facts pertaining to the selection and training of the executioner must remain confidential'. Healthcare personnel help make lethal executions 'humane', 'faster', and perhaps constitutional. Death penalty states appropriate healthcare personnel to alleviate the pain of death or to offer the illusion of alleviating pain. If punishment was once harsh, it is now peaceful and painless. Maryland's penitentiary historian states that 'the worst physical pain' from lethal injection is 'the prick of a needle'. Arizona's historical fact sheet on the death penalty similarly dismisses the possibility of pain from a lethal injection, and describes the pain a prisoner feels from lethal gas as akin to a heart attack. 'Death by lethal injection is not painful and the inmate goes to sleep prior to the fatal effects of the Pavulon and Potassium Chloride' [according to Arizona's statute].

The Kansas statute makes clear that healthcare personnel—whether called a 'nurse' or a 'physician'—are important because of the knowledge they have and the image they project. Their execution activities disperse power and responsibility throughout the prison complex, mirroring developments in civil society regarding decentralization. According to [Minneapolis attorney John D.] Bessler, the multilayered process of social and coercive control regarding the means of punishment has gotten so complex that 'no one in the entire criminal justice system is now fully accountable for death sentences'. Focusing on the rationalization of punishment, [New York University law professor David] Garland adds that penal agents today 'avoid the bad conscience and cultural infamy that used to attach to the executioner or the jailer by claiming to be more than merely instruments of punishment.

> *Various states indemnify the healthcare personnel involved in executing prisoners.*

From the standpoint of lethal injections, the 'agent of welfare', in [scholar Michel] Foucault's words, the nurse or the physician, is less necessary than what she or he represents: the care of the soul in the care of the state. Their purpose is to transform executions from being terrifying to being peaceful and to render submissive the condemned prisoner. In the process, their work, too, is transformed. They heal by pacifying, not correcting. Their work is legal fiction. Under a mask of care, healthcare professionals (and the nursing and medical technologies that surround an execution) combine part of the state's power and disciplinary knowledge (nursing and medicine) in order to achieve their work. . . .

The changing face of the executioner

Over time, the face of the executioner has changed. When we think about these persons we might imagine them wearing a hood, 'hiding in the shadow of the gallows'. In Florida, which uses the electric chair to execute prisoners, the executioner remains hooded throughout the death process. 'You won't be seeing him', a Florida Department of Corrections official told a journalist; 'Not on this side of life'. [According to scholar R. Johnson,]

> The image of the executioner as a sinister and often solitary person, is, of course, a holdover from

earlier times, when executions were public and executioners were scorned as evil, contaminated by the death work that was their livelihood. . . . They were often afforded a hood or cloak while at work to protect their identities, which would offer them a token shield against harm. Some of these execution traditions, or at least remnants of them, linger on even today. Thus it is that a few states hire freelance executioners and engage in macabre theatrics. Executioners may be picked up under cover of darkness at lonely country crossroads; some still wear black hoods to hide their identity. They slip into the prison unnoticed, do their work, then return to their civilian lives.

Yet this is not entirely descriptive of the reality of the death process. A review of prison literature informs us that healthcare professionals are part of the 'execution team'. The sinister figure of the hooded executioner has been replaced by the 'caring' figure of a healthcare professional. Not only do healthcare professionals participate in the administration of the death penalty, they are involved in the torture or corporal punishment of prisoners in other countries. As violations of human rights have become more pervasive in prisons, scientific discoveries have brought about more sophisticated forms of torture, methods of resuscitation and execution. For example, Amnesty International reports that 'lethal injection executions depend on medical drugs and procedures and the potential of this kind of execution to involve medical professionals in unethical behavior, including direct involvement in killing, is clear'. In the United States, healthcare professionals' participation in executions receives the legal protection, which includes shielding their identity from public scrutiny. Arizona's capital punishment statute, which calls for 'an intravenous injection of a substance or substances in a lethal quantity sufficient to cause death', shields healthcare personnel from legal retribution. 'If a person who participates or performs ancillary functions in an execution is licensed by a board the licensing board shall not suspend or revoke the person's license as a result of the person's participation in an execution'. Illinois's statute is more explicit: 'Notwithstanding any other provision of law, assistance, participation in, or the performance of ancillary or other functions pursuant to this Section, including but not limited to the administration of the lethal substance or substances required by this Section, shall not be construed to constitute the practice of medicine'.

❝Nurses who participate either directly or indirectly in legally authorized execution violate [the] nursing code of ethics.❞

The state enlists healthcare professionals, mainly nurses and physicians, to select lethal injection sites, start intravenous lines to serve as ports for lethal injections, inspect, test, or maintain lethal injection devices, consult with or supervise lethal injection personnel and participate directly in the administration of the lethal solution. Healthcare knowledge is crucial for the performance of the new killing technique of lethal injection. This latest discovery in the killing arsenal, which is considered more humane than electrocution because it does less damage to the prisoner's body, is an obvious application of scientific (medical and para-medical) knowledge and professional skills. [Director Steven] Trombley describes the process as follows:

> The inmate walks from the holding cell to the gurney, accompanied by guards and he is placed in a supine position on the gurney and he is strapped. Legs, abdomen, chest. . . . The arm that takes the IV [intravenous line] is exposed. The nurse-anesthetist, who acts like a nurse consultant, starts the IV. Using a number 16-gauge needle, and a plastic catheter . . . [after a signal to begin] they press the button [of the lethal injection machine]. . . . The first solution, sodium pentothal, goes into the person. He's awake, and then he goes to sleep. [After another minute] the Pavulon . . . is injected, and it arrests the respiratory muscles. Paralyze the lungs and depress the respiratory center. . . . You can see the patient doing an agonal, or terminal, breathing. . . . Finally the potassium chloride is given and it's three times the lethal dose. . . . When the prisoner had died and had been certified as such, the nurse-anesthetist re-

moves the IV. Then the mortician comes in and removes him from the gurney to his table, and takes him to the funeral parlor.

The official positions of American nursing academics regarding capital punishment are unknown. But for the International Council of Nurses (ICN) and the American Nurses Association (ANA), it is clear that participation in execution is contrary to the 'ethical traditions of the nursing profession'. Moreover, the ANA states that regardless of personal opinion, nurses who participate either directly or indirectly in legally authorized execution violate [the] nursing code of ethics.

> The ANA is strongly opposed to all forms of participation, by whatever means, whether under civil or military legal authority. Nurses should refrain from participation in capital punishment and not take part in assessment, supervision or monitoring of the procedure or the prisoner; procuring, prescribing or preparing medications or solutions; inserting the intravenous catheter; injecting the lethal solution; and attending or witnessing the execution as a nurse. The fact that capital punishment is currently supported in many segments of society does not override the obligation of nurses to uphold the ethical mandates of the profession.

The deathwatch

According to the International Council of Nurses, nursing educators should address issues related to capital punishment and torture. ICN advocates that all levels of nursing education curricula include the recognition of human rights issues and violations, such as the death penalty and torture and awareness of the use of medical technology for executions.

Organizations to Contact

The editors have compiled the following list of organizations concerned with the issues debated in this book. The descriptions are derived from materials provided by the organizations. All have publications or information available for interested readers. The list was compiled on the date of publication of the present volume; the information provided here may change. Be aware that many organizations take several weeks or longer to respond to inquiries, so allow as much time as possible.

American Civil Liberties Union (ACLU)
Capital Punishment Project
125 Broad St., 18th Fl., New York, NY 10004
(212) 549-2500 • fax: (212) 549-2646
Web site: www.aclu.org

The ACLU believes that capital punishment violates the Constitution's ban on cruel and unusual punishment as well as the requirements of due process and equal protection under the law. Its Capital Punishment Project is dedicated to abolishing the death penalty. It publishes and distributes numerous books and pamphlets, including *The Case Against the Death Penalty* and *Frequently Asked Questions Concerning the Writ of Habeas Corpus and the Death Penalty*.

Amnesty International USA (AI)
Program to Abolish the Death Penalty
322 Eighth Ave., 10th Fl., New York, NY 10001
(212) 633-4280 • fax: (212) 627-1451
e-mail: mundies@aiusa.org • Web site: www.amnesty-usa.org/abolish

Amnesty International's Program to Abolish the Death Penalty seeks the abolishment of the death penalty worldwide. Its most recent activities have been aimed toward decreasing the use of the death penalty internationally, including in the United States, and increasing the number of countries that have removed the death penalty as an option for punishment. It also serves as advocate in individual clemency cases. Several times a year, it publishes *The Death Penalty: List of Abolitionist and Retentionist Countries* and *Facts and Figures on the Death Penalty*, reports of gathered information on the death penalty worldwide.

Campaign to End the Death Penalty (CEDP)
PO Box 25730, Chicago, IL 60625
(773) 955-4841
Web site: www.nodeathpenalty.org/index.html

A nonprofit organization actively attempting to abolish the death penalty. Its Web site contains local contact information, regular updates on death row cases, and fact sheets about capital punishment in the United States. The CEDP regularly publishes a newsletter, *The New Abolitionist*.

Canadian Coalition Against the Death Penalty (CCADP)
PO Box 38104, 550 Eglinton Ave. W, Toronto, ON M5N 3A8 Canada
(416) 693-9112 • fax: (416) 686-1630
e-mail: ccadp@home.com • Web site: www.ccadp.org

CCADP is a not-for-profit international human rights organization dedicated to educating on alternatives to the death penalty worldwide and
to providing emotional and practical support to death row inmates, their
families, and the families of murder victims. The center releases pamphlets and periodic press releases, and its Web site includes a student re-
source center providing research information on capital punishment.

Catholics Against Capital Punishment (CACP)
PO Box 3125, Arlington, VA 22203-8125
(301) 652-1125 • fax: (301) 652-1125
Web site: www2.dcci.com/ltlflwr/CACP.html

Founded in 1992 to promote the Catholic Church's teachings about
capital punishment, Catholics Against Capital Punishment is a national
organization that works to stop the death penalty in the United States.
The *CACP News Notes* is published four to six times a year.

Death Penalty Information Center (DPIC)
1320 Eighteenth St. NW, 5th Fl., Washington, DC 20036
(202) 293-6970 • fax: (202) 822-4787
e-mail: dpic@essential.org • Web site: www.deathpenaltyinfo.org

DPIC opposes the death penalty because it believes that capital punishment is discriminatory, costly to taxpayers, and may result in innocent
persons being put to death. It publishes many reports yearly about public views on the death penalty.

Justice Fellowship (JF)
PO Box 16069, Washington, DC 20041-6069
(703) 904-7312 • fax: (703) 478-9679
Web site: www.justicefellowship.org

This Christian organization bases its work for reform of the justice system on the concept of victim-offender reconciliation. It does not take a
position on the death penalty, but it publishes the pamphlet *Capital
Punishment: A Call to Dialogue.*

Justice for All (JFA)
PO Box 55159, Houston, TX 77255
(713) 935-9300 • fax: (713) 935-9301
e-mail: info@jfa.net • Web site: www.jfa.net

Justice for All is a not-for-profit criminal justice reform organization
that supports the death penalty. Its activities include publishing the
monthly newsletter *The Voice of Justice* and circulating online petitions
to keep violent offenders from being paroled early.

Lamp of Hope Project
PO Box 305, League City, TX 77574-0305
e-mail: aspanhel@airmail.net • Web site: www.lampofhope.org

The project was established and is run primarily by Texas death row inmates. It works for victim-offender reconciliation and for the protection of the civil rights of prisoners, particularly the right of habeas corpus appeal. It publishes and distributes the periodical *Texas Death Row Journal*.

Lincoln Institute for Research and Education
1001 Connecticut Ave. NW, Suite 1135, Washington, DC 20036
(202) 223-5112

The institute is a conservative think tank that studies public policy issues affecting the lives of black Americans, including the issue of the death penalty, which it favors. It publishes the quarterly *Lincoln Review*.

National Coalition to Abolish the Death Penalty (NCADP)
1436 U St. NW, Suite 104, Washington, DC 20009
(202) 387-3890 • fax: (202) 387-5590
e-mail: info@ncadp • Web site: www.ncadp.org

The National Coalition to Abolish the Death Penalty is a collection of more than 115 groups working together to stop executions in the United States. The organization compiles statistics on the death penalty. To further its goal, the coalition publishes *Legislative Action to Abolish the Death Penalty*, information packets, pamphlets, and research materials.

National Criminal Justice Reference Service (NCJRS)
U.S. Department of Justice
PO Box 6000, Rockville, MD 20849-6000
(301) 519-5500 • (800) 851-3420
e-mail: askncjrs@ncjrs.org • Web site: www.ncjrs.org

The National Criminal Justice Reference Service is one of the most extensive sources of information on criminal and juvenile justice in the world. For a nominal fee, this clearinghouse provides topical searches and reading lists on many areas of criminal justice, including the death penalty. It publishes an annual report on capital punishment.

Bibliography

Books

Stuart Banner · *The Death Penalty: An American History.* Cambridge, MA: Harvard University Press, 2002.

Hugo Adam Bedau and Paul G. Cassell · *Debating the Death Penalty: Should America Have Capital Punishment? The Experts on Both Sides Make Their Best Case.* New York: Oxford University Press, 2004.

Walter Berns · *For Capital Punishment: Crime and the Morality of the Death Penalty.* Lanham, MD: University Press of America, 1991.

Alan I. Bigel · *Justices William J. Brennan Jr. and Thurgood Marshall on Capital Punishment: Its Constitutionality, Morality, Deterrent Effect, and Interpretation by the Court.* Lanham, MD: University Press of America, 1997.

Robert M. Bohm · *Deathquest: An Introduction to the Theory and Practice of Capital Punishment in the United States.* Cincinnati: Anderson, 1999.

David R. Dow and Mark Dow · *Machinery of Death: The Reality of America's Death Penalty Regime.* New York: Routledge, 2002.

Benjamin Fleury-Steiner · *Jurors' Stories of Death: How America's Death Penalty Invests in Inequality.* Ann Arbor: University of Michigan Press, 2004.

Herbert H. Haines · *Against Capital Punishment: The Anti–Death Penalty Movement in America, 1972–1994.* New York: Oxford University Press, 1996.

Enid Harlow et al., eds. · *The Machinery of Death: A Shocking Indictment of Capital Punishment in the United States.* New York: Amnesty International USA, 1995.

Roger Hood · *The Death Penalty: A Worldwide Perspective.* 3rd ed. New York: Oxford University Press, 2002.

Jesse Jackson · *Legal Lynching: Racism, Injustice, and the Death Penalty.* New York: Marlowe, 1996.

Robert Jay Lifton · *Who Owns Death? Capital Punishment, the American Conscience, and the End of Executions.* New York: Morrow, 2000.

Kathleen O'Shea · *Women and the Death Penalty in the United States, 1900–1998.* Westport, CT: Praeger, 1999.

Ivan Solotaroff · *The Last Face You'll Ever See: The Private Life of the American Death Penalty.* New York: HarperCollins, 2001.

Periodicals

D. Aarons	"Can Inordinate Delay Between a Death Sentence and Execution Constitute Cruel and Unusual Punishment?" *Seton Hall Law Review*, vol. 29, no. 1, 1998.
J.R. Ackerand and C.S. Lanier	"Unfit to Live, Unfit to Die: Incompetency for Execution Under Modern Death Penalty Legislation," *Criminal Law Bulletin*, vol. 33, no. 2, 1997.
Jonathan Alter	"The Death Penalty on Trial," *Newsweek*, June 12, 2000.
Atlantic Monthly	"The Facts of Death," May 2004.
Walter Berns and Joseph Bessette	"Why the Death Penalty Is Fair," *Wall Street Journal*, January 9, 1998.
Thom Brooks	"Retributivist Arguments Against Capital Punishment," *Journal of Social Philosophy*, June 2004.
William Glaberson	"Death Penalty: Court Roster May Be Key to Its Future," *New York Times*, June 26, 2004.
Christopher Hitchens	"Scenes from an Execution," *Vanity Fair*, January 1998.
Anne James and Joanne Cecil	"Out of Step: Juvenile Death Penalty in the United States," *International Journal of Children's Rights*, vol. 12, no. 3, July 2004.
Laura I. Langbein	"Politics, Rules, and Death Row: Why States Eschew or Execute Executions," *Social Science Quarterly*, vol. 80, no. 4, 1999.
Brooke A. Masters	"Death Row to Freedom: A Journey Ends," *Washington Post*, February 13, 2001.
Colman McCarthy	"Insane and on Death Row," *Washington Post*, May 6, 1995.
National Catholic Reporter	"Dissent and the Death Penalty," July 2, 2004.
G. Potter	"Crime Control and the Death Penalty," *Advocate*, vol. 19, no. 6, 1997.
Anna Quindlen	"The High Cost of Death," *New York Times*, November 19, 1994.
Eric Reitan	"Why the Deterrence Argument for Capital Punishment Fails," *Criminal Justice Ethics*, vol. 12, no. 1, 1993.
Michael B. Ross	"It's Time for Me to Die: An Inside Look at Death Row," *Journal of Psychiatry and Law*, vol. 26, no. 4, 1998.
Jon Sorensen et al.	"Capital Punishment and Deterrence: Examining the Effect of Executions on Murder in Texas," *Crime and Delinquency*, vol. 45, no. 4, 1999.

USA Today	"Death Penalty Is Fitting Punishment for Many Crimes," June 4, 2004.
USA Today	"Let Death Penalty Die," June 1, 2004.
Henry Weinstein	"Death Penalty Debate—Can New Violence Be Predicted?" *Los Angeles Times*, November 6, 2000.
John T. Whitehead et al.	"Elite Versus Citizen Attitudes on Capital Punishment: Incongruity Between the Public and Policymakers," *Journal of Criminal Justice*, vol. 27, no. 3, 1999.
DeWayne Wickham	"U.S. Sets Poor Example When It Comes to Death Penalty," *USA Today*, April 14, 2004.

Web Sites

American Society of Criminology (ASC)
Division on Critical Criminology
http://sun.soci.niu.edu/~critcrim/dp/dp.html

The ASC Division on Critical Criminology is committed to studying the way that society handles crime and criminals. They have determined that the death penalty is unjust because it is racist and does not deter crime. Their Web site contains fact sheets, essays, and reports that argue for and against the death penalty.

Capital Defense Weekly
http://capitaldefenseweekly.com/briefbank.html

A large clearinghouse that includes capital punishment case law, news, and litigation resources, as well as materials for death penalty activists.

***Frontline:* Angel on Death Row**
www.pbs.org/wgbh/pages/frontline/angel

Frontline, an investigative arm of PBS, profiles anti–death penalty activist Sister Helen Prejean, author of *Dead Man Walking*, and the death penalty debate in the United States. The Web site contains pro and con death penalty arguments, access to streaming video interviews, and a time line of the death penalty throughout history.

Pro-Death Penalty.com
www.prodeathpenalty.com

One of several Web sites created by Justice for All, a volunteer, nonprofit organization founded in 1992 to serve as an advocate for American citizens seeking justice. This site provides articles, fact sheets, and research in support of the death penalty, including lists of people currently on death row and their victims, interviews with prominent death penalty advocates, and current news about capital punishment cases across America.

Index